A Decorator's Tales
By The Yard

A Decorator's Tales By The Yard

Memoirs of a New Jersey Decorator

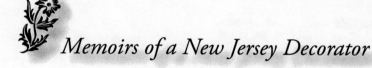

Roseann Kearney

authorHOUSE®

AuthorHouse™
1663 Liberty Drive
Bloomington, IN 47403
www.authorhouse.com
Phone: 1-800-839-8640

First published by AuthorHouse   09/28/2011

ISBN: 978-1-4670-4255-0 (hc)
ISBN: 978-1-4670-4254-3 (ebk)

Library of Congress Control Number: 2011917317

Printed in the United States of America

Table of Contents

EDICATION

To my Houston Stone, You are my Angel. You are the stars in my sky; the shine in my eyes and every morning when I wake up you will be the beat of my heart and remember you will always be my little cowboy. I love you very much and you will always be in my heart.

To my Biff, my faithful little friend who sat at my side day and night while I wrote this book. Thank you for your devotion and love.

To my children, Scott, Stacey and Shawn, my grandchildren, Austin, Dallas, Mackenzie, Madisyn and Colt. Thank you for sharing me with so many other families.

My CHILDHOOD, MY HOME, MY STYLE, MY PHILOSOPHY

I grew up in Jersey City; where I lived with my dad, Pete, my mom, Anita, also known as Nettie, and my brother Peter.

My parents owned a very modest home on Charles Street that they bought for $10,000 way back when. The old original kitchen had a wood burning stove that heated the house. We would wake up in the morning freezing, get dressed as fast as possible and run into the kitchen where we ate our breakfast in our coats in front of the stove to keep warm until my parents saved enough money to convert to oil heat.

My dad owned a taxi business and my mom worked two jobs. She worked in a children's clothing store and also in a fabric store. They both worked very hard so we could live a good life, live in a nice home and get a good education. We always had beautiful clothes, music lessons and always went to the Jersey shore for a week in the summer with Uncle Angelo, Aunt Elsie and my cousins Carolyn and Maureen.

Growing up in Jersey City was very different from the way kids grow up today. My brother Peter and his friends played stickball in the street, while I made dollhouses out of shoeboxes. I would play for hours with that shoebox and my mom would help me decorate it. I went shopping on the avenue with my friends. We were allowed to go to the movie theatre without our parents. We knew all the neighbors. It was a real safe neighborhood and we had lots of friends.

But, the thing I remember most is my home. We never had an abundance of money, but my mom had the greatest taste. Our home always looked like a "Showplace". When neighbors went for a walk and passed our house, they would stop to admire my mother's front garden and her front bay window that was always decorated so beautifully. I remember people saying, "Nettie, could I come in to see your house?"

My mother was always very proud of her house and would happily show it. My mom made her own window treatments. This is where I saw my first version of the balloon curtain. (My mom should have patented it.)

My uncles, aunts and cousins would flock to our house. They all had more money than we did but for some reason, they always enjoyed being at our house and they especially loved my mother's great, homemade Italian cooking. Homemade raviolis about 8" long by 3" were her specialty. Meatballs, braciole, there was always tons of food and lots of very noisy people.

I'm glad I paid a lot of attention to what my mom did in our house. She was my first teacher and I learned so much about decorating from her. She had a knack of making everything look beautiful. She was a trendsetter.

Every Monday night, my brother, Peter and I would rush to get our homework done because we knew we were allowed to stay up until nine o'clock to watch "I Love Lucy". This was a special treat. Those were the good old days.

Today I live in Bergen County, New Jersey, in a 30 year old, white, center-hall colonial. Times have changed. Life isn't quite as quiet and simple as it was back then. We rarely see a neighbor; people don't walk past our house. Everyone, including myself, jumps into their cars to get wherever they have to go. Life is so much faster. I get up at 6 o'clock every morning. I'm off to my first client by 8 o'clock.

Thank God, I love what I do, but I'm always running. If I'm not shopping for furniture or carpeting or kitchen cabinets, I'm running someplace for a fabric sample or designing a piece of furniture or installing a window treatment. When I get home at night, I open the front door, kick off my shoes and I thank God that I'm home. Home Sweet Home!

Everyday I'm in one beautiful home after the other. Homes that are published in magazines, big homes, little homes, mini mansions, apartments, condos and vacation homes on the ocean. I see them all, but when I come home at night I still love my HOME best. My house is very special to me. It's warm, it's cozy, it's elegant, it's child friendly. It's many things and I truly love it.

When you enter my front hall, you walk into a milk chocolate colored, Damask wall covered room with cream-colored trim. I'm relaxed as soon as I enter. On the left of the entrance hall is my living room and dining room. These rooms are formal with darker brown walls, brown silk custom furniture, a beautiful custom made fireplace with lots of interesting accessories and cream-colored flokati rugs in both rooms. In the evening when I'm entertaining I light candles and they set off a soft warm glow. These rooms are very enchanting.

My family room is on the other side of the hall. This room is also brown. The ceiling is also hand painted to look like an old tin ceiling. My furniture is soft and cuddly, filled with down. People sit on it and they never want to leave. I especially love it when we have a warm fire glowing from the fireplace. While sitting in the family room, you are able to look right into the music room. The only pieces of furniture in this room are my black, baby grand piano and my antique, iron music stand that I found while antiquing. Tons of pictures of my family sit on my piano along with plants and a lovely purple orchid that was sent to me by my brother Peter and his wife Sharon.

MY KITCHEN. Everyone wants to hang out in my kitchen. The walls are painted white in a Venetian Plaster. The ceiling has old-fashioned anaglypta wallpaper painted in a clay color. We eat at a very large old country pine table with cherry red chairs. The black and cream toile fabric hangs on the side of the window just to add a little color and warmth but doesn't block the view of my Victorian deck, garden and pool. On the far left side of the kitchen sits an old antique pine library filled with all kinds of children's books. My grandchildren love to sit on an old pine bench reading for hours.

On the same side as the bench and the library I have a very whimsical, life-size statue of a French pastry chef. He carries a basket filled with all kinds of French bread and rolls and some flowers. One day my faux painter, Jeremy stopped by the house and when he saw the statue, he thought it looked just like Lou my old slipcover man. I told him not to mention it to him. I didn't want to hurt his feelings because this statue was pretty funny looking. A few days later, my contractor, Hector stopped by. He took a look at the statue and said the same thing. Again I told him not to tease Lou about this because I didn't want to hurt his feelings. About a week later, Lou came to the house. He took one look at the statue and said, "This is the ugliest guy I ever saw," and laughed.

I like to have whimsical pieces mixed in the right spot. It's light and fun and everyone enjoys it. My kitchen is a fun place to hang out in and I think it reflects a part of my personality.

I love my deck! It's so peaceful. I sometimes get up early in the morning. I grab a blanket and I go outside and lay on a big old Victorian wicker chaise lounge that I have had for years. I love to go out early in the morning to listen to the silence and then the birds seem to suddenly wake up and start chirping and singing in the trees.

My porch wraps around the back of the house. It's painted white, a touch of Victorian and a touch of the tropics, with palm trees and plants and all kinds of flowers. It is completely covered with a white, canvas canopy, which enables us to be out there, rain or shine. I enjoy sitting out there with my family and friends.

The deck is surrounded with multi colored hydrangea plants, white and pink dogwood trees and magnolia bushes that smell like a fine perfume. My guests always enjoy the porch and garden. They say, "Who needs to go on vacation. You have your own resort right here." This is a place where I relax, where I sometimes go to think, where I entertain, read a book, write and sometimes paint a picture. This is my very own Shangri-La!

As much as I love the deck, I have one area of the house that I love even more and this is my BEDROOM. My bedroom is my own intimate retreat. My bedroom is quiet, rather sparse with only a few pieces of furniture. I think it is soft and romantic. This is where I go to get away from everything. I have a big, old, bronze colored iron bed always covered in crisp ivory sheets and a linen, ivory monogrammed duvet cover. My bed is very fluffy and when I'm exhausted at night I feel like a princess when I retreat to my big, soft, feather bed.

The walls and ceiling are painted in a soft, milkshake brown, colored paint, Hillsborough beige from Benjamin Moore. The color is especially soothing. I recommend it all the time. On the side of the bed are two round tables covered in ivory damask fabric. I didn't want any heavy pieces in my room. My chaise sits in a corner of my room with a white mink throw on it. It's so nice to cuddle on a cool winter day. Behind the chaise stands a very slim, Victorian Christmas tree, decorated in ivory roses and ivory satin ribbons. This stays up all year round. A cream-colored secretary sits on the wall in front of my bed. The only other thing in my room is an iron pedestal between my two front widows. A cream vase sits on top with a bunch of white dogwood branches. On the shelf below are my decorating books that I love to browse through.

As my life grows busier and everything is so noisy around me, I look forward to returning to my quiet retreat to get nourished for the next day's work. This room, more than any other, defines my style. I believe that my house is unique. I guess I'm not the typical decorator or designer. I have always broken all the rules. I believe there are no special rules when you are designing. When it comes to good design, be unique, be different. Go to a store and buy something that is not so pretty and turn it into something beautiful and special. That's what will make your home stand out from the rest.

I guess that MY PHILOSOPHY PERTAINING TO DECORATING AND DESIGN is the same as my philosophy in life. Enjoy decorating your home, even if it's just painting a room. Select a color that you know you will love to live with. Don't be afraid to make a decision. A million other people do not have to like it or agree with you as long as you love it.

Everyone has a different style and different likes and dislikes. When a new client calls me and wants me to copy something that she saw someplace else, I usually refuse to do it. You shouldn't copy someone else's ideas. Create your home so it becomes your own. It's so wonderful knowing that your home or room is different from everyone else's. Make it yours.

I know that when I'm decorating for myself; I need a no-fuss, easy style, nothing overdone. I have lots of styles that I like, but I know, in my home, I need a very peaceful environment because I'm solving everyone else's problems all day. When I'm not at work, I need to come home to peace and quiet. I thank God for my home.

NTRODUCTION

In the beginning, there was nothing. Then God created the sky, the birds, the flowers and of course, people.

Every time I begin a new decorating project, I can't help but think of the beginning. Along with my very talented contractors, I try to create an environment that makes my clients happy.

I consider myself so fortunate to be able to create a sky, a landscape, a garden room, a barn or a castle, anything my client desires. I work with the best, well-known artists, furniture designers, architects and builders to make my client's dreams become a reality.

I have been decorating over thirty years and I have been so lucky to have worked in so many beautiful homes with so many wonderful people

Decorating has offered me the opportunity to do exactly what I love to do most, to shop without spending my own money, and to make people happy. Who could ask for more?

When I decorate someone's home, I become very close to them and become part of their lives. Sometimes I feel as if I have become a member of their family. I become their doctor, lawyer, their friend and especially their listener.

In most cases, when I am decorating a home I am with the people for a while. Even a small decorating job could involve being with the client three to six months. Sometimes depending on the job, this involvement could last for several years. Long after a job is completed, my clients call me to get a piece of furniture, a carpet, a painting or to re-do a room, or sometimes just to have lunch or dinner. Some of my clients have been calling me for over thirty years.

In the process of doing this work, I have made some very long-lasting and loving friendships and I have been touched in so many ways. I have celebrated engagements, weddings, communions, births and unfortunately, some deaths.

I have worked in thousands of homes and businesses in the New Jersey and New York area. I have also worked in other states. When my clients move or buy a vacation home, I am the first person they call to check it out. I have worked all over Florida; Pennsylvania; Boulder, Colorado; Williamsburg, Virginia; Rhode Island; Maryland; the Ritz Carlton in Washington, D.C. and numerous homes at the Jersey shore.

My clients are used to working with me, they know my style and I think more than anything else they trust me with their homes. They know that I would treat their home like it was my own.

I believe the most important part of decorating is creating a place where my clients, their families and friends can relax. A place where they never want to leave, a place they are proud of, a place they feel warm and safe in and most of all a place they call home. This is a huge responsibility. I feel so honored and blessed that so many people have allowed me to enter their homes and become such an important part of their lives.

In the thirty-three years that I have been in the business I have been telling my friends and family stories about my clients. For just as many years, these same people have been telling me to write a book in order to share these stories with other people. In most of the stories I have changed the names, to protect the innocent, me!

Well, here it is. I have finally done it. I hope you enjoy reading about these folks, as much as I enjoyed working with them and remembering them. They have definitely, made my life fuller.

Please put this book on your cocktail table and share it with your friends and family. I have had a fantastic time writing it and hope you will enjoy A DECORATOR'S TALES BY THE YARD!

TALES

TALES CONTINUED

"Home Sweet Home."

REMEMBERING REBECCA

It was September 1991 when I first met the Mikasa family. When I walked into the entrance hall of their lovely home, I knew instantly that someone very special lived there.

Mrs. Mikasa was a warm, friendly lady with the nicest, bubbly smile and one of the warmest laughs that I have ever heard. Mr. Mikasa, also a very sweet man with a wonderful sense of humor and a very kind thoughtful nature. They were both very sensitive special people but the special one I am speaking of is Rebecca.

I never had the pleasure of meeting her because she died in 1988. She was one of the 270 innocent people who were killed in the terrorist bombing of Pan Am flight 103 over Lockerbie, Scotland. Rebecca was only 20 years old. She was young, vibrant and intelligent with lots of talent and a dream of becoming a photojournalist. She was a Newhouse photojournalist student at Syracuse University.

She was returning home for the holidays after spending her junior year at Syracuse University London Center studying, when she became the victim of the terrorist bombing. It was Christmas time, the twenty first of December 1988 when this terrible tragedy took place. The family was waiting for Rebecca so that they could celebrate Christmas together. Mrs. Mikasa told me "Christmas will never again be the same without Rebecca." Being a mother of three myself, I could understand her feelings losing this beautiful child.

Although I never personally met Rebecca, there is no possible way of not knowing her instantly. From the minute I walked into their home I felt I knew her. Her magnificent photographs hang in the entrance hall as well as in every other room.

When you enter the beautiful, green faux marble library, the first thing you see is a large, lovely photograph of beautiful Rebecca. Her beautiful dark hair and sparkling, big brown eyes welcome you into the room. This picture is lit at all times in her memory.

As I looked at this photograph, I saw the same warm smile and I could almost hear that same, very special bubbly laugh that her mother has. Rebecca is definitely a mystical presence within the house.

Mrs. Mikasa told me that the family always loved the Christmas season but they had never before decorated the exterior of the house or the entrance hall. This year they decided to go all out because Rebecca would be coming home. The entrance had lovely flower garlands on the magnificent staircase and the exterior was so pretty that the town awarded them a prize for the best decorated home. They were so happy that Rebecca was returning. They wanted everything to be perfect. Never did they think when they were preparing for this that they would be having a funeral instead of a Christmas celebration.

Mr. and Mrs. Mikasa are probably two of the grandest human beings that I ever met and worked with. They are warm, kind, intelligent and they always have a smile on their faces. Even though they lost their precious child, a gift that was given to them by God and taken away so quickly and so senselessly, they remain kind to everyone.

I am writing about the family because I am honored to have had the great opportunity to meet Rebecca through her mother and father and through her wonderful photography.

This unique, very special family is making sure that Rebecca is remembered. I know that I can't get her out of my mind and my heart. I see those lovely eyes, her beautiful dark hair and that warm smile right in front of me. Although I did not know her personally, I know I will always remember Rebecca.

THE DIRTY OLD MAN

I've been married for the past 34 years. I've never had the desire to be with any other man and I've never had a man hit on me, until recently. I wouldn't want to get anyone in trouble, so lets just call this person Mr. B.

I had been working with Mr. and Mrs. B for about 6 months when I had an evening meeting with a contractor at their house to go over the plans for their very small powder room. They were both waiting for me when I arrived and they followed me into the room to see what I had planned for that area.

The three of us were stuffed into this little room like sardines. When Mrs. B left us to answer the doorbell, Mr. B grabbed me, kissed me on the lips and told me he wanted me to meet him in the city some night.

"We could have a great time together, Roseann," he breathed on me as he spoke in his Henny Youngman voice.

When Mrs. B returned to continue going over the plans, I found I could hardly speak. I only wanted to get out of that room and out of that house as quickly as I could. I excused myself and went outdoors for some fresh air.

For some strange reason, that overweight, bald, obnoxious man in his 60's had made me feel sick to my stomach.

Now you have to understand, I was no young chick. I was 48 years old, a little overweight and as I already said, happily married. Knowing what we look like, you can better imagine the position I was now in.

I had a few choices.

I didn't want to go back into that powder room with him breathing all over me.

I didn't want to tell Mrs. B about her husband's behavior. Who knew if she would believe me? I didn't want to jeopardize my job. Oh what the hell, I didn't need it that badly.

I took a deep breath and returned to the house. I told them I didn't feel well and would come back another time, thinking to myself that that would be when Romeo wasn't around. This seemed simple enough because I knew he worked long hours and was seldom there. It felt like a sensible and safe decision that would avoid contact with Mr. B. I was wrong.

A few nights later, I was awakened by the ringing phone. I had been fast asleep, even though it was only 11 o'clock. When I answered the call, I heard, "Hello Roseann," and immediately recognized the Henny Youngman voice.

When I answered, "Hello Mr. B," he was delighted that I recognized his voice, and for a second time, invited me to meet him in the city for dinner.

As nicely as I could, I said, "What a lovely invitation. My husband and I would be happy to accept. Will Mrs. B be joining us?"

"My wife? Of course, not. You know she annoys me, Roseann. She's a terrible old bitch and she's driving me crazy. I hope you don't think I have anything harmful in mind. I just find you a delightful person and very soothing."

"Mr. B, an ice cream pop is soothing, I'm not. I can't discuss your wife with you. You never should have kissed me when I was at your house and I don't want you to call me again unless it has to do with the work I'm doing for you and Mrs. B."

Two weeks later, Mrs. B called to say that she would be away for a month's vacation on some island or other. It wasn't unusual for them to take separate vacations. "I need some relaxation and time away from Mr. B and all his arguing."

I certainly didn't blame her, and was thrilled when she said I could wait until she returned to continue the work on the house. She said Mr. B had offered to let me in the house early each day before he left for work. I told her I would decline his sweet offer. The decision to have some time away from the crazy house made my day.

But of course he called again the following week "Don't hang up, Roseann, I need to talk to you about the house."

"Mr. B, Mrs. B and I agreed I wouldn't be doing any work in her absence."

"I know, I know, but I can't stand living this way with all the furniture piled in the family room. If you come over and tell me where to put everything, I'm sure I can move it myself."

He wouldn't take "no" for an answer, so you can imagine his surprise when I showed up at his house that evening with my 27 year old son! I told him I thought he could use help moving the furniture.

He said he appreciated the help, but he was sure he could have managed alone as long as I told him where to put it.

The truth is, I would have liked to tell him where to put it, but I am a professional.

My son and I had a good laugh on our way home, especially when he asked me if Mr. B reminded me of Henny Youngman.

I decided not to return for any future projects. When Mrs. B called me to do another project recently, I told her I was too busy and couldn't take on any more clients. Sometimes, it's just not worth taking the job!

"It's warm, cozy, it's elegant."

HAUNTED HOUSES

I personally don't believe in haunted houses or ghosts but I have clients that do.

Let me explain, one day I was with a new client returning from a New York City showroom. I didn't know the client very well. I was trying to make small talk.

The day before, I had read in the newspaper that there was a haunted house for sale in Nyack, New York. "Why would anyone advertise that their house was haunted? Who would want to buy it?" My new client responded without any hesitation and said "I would! I would buy a haunted house in a second."

As I mentioned, I didn't know this client very well so I wasn't quite sure if she was serious or joking but she seemed like she really meant it. She went on to tell me that the last house she owned in Westwood, New Jersey was haunted. "Your house was haunted?" I responded. She went on to tell me that whenever she or her husband would put something like their keys on the hall table, they would mysteriously disappear. At first they thought they put the keys down someplace else in the house but they finally realized that something strange was going on.

One day as she entered the hall looking for her keys she became so frustrated that she started to scream aloud. "What's going on? Where are my keys?" As she looked up, she saw two old men standing in the hall, holding her keys. She asked who they were and what were they doing in her house. They told her that the house was theirs. They had lived in it for the past 55 years and they were a part of it.

They went on to say that they meant her no harm. They wanted to make sure that the new owners loved the house as much as they did and that she would take good care of it. "Of course, I love it," she said. And she told them that she would take very good care of the house for them. They dropped the keys on the steps and they disappeared. I, of

9

course, sat in the car probably with my mouth open, wondering if she believed what she told me or if she had a drinking problem. I thought to myself, this job was really going to be interesting.

As I sat there bewildered, she continued to tell me that one night, when her and her husband were entertaining some friends, suddenly everyone in the room turned their heads to the left at the same time. She had been busy getting drinks and snacks for everyone so she just caught the last second of this unusual sight. She asked what happened and the guests, told her that her black cat just ran past the fireplace. She told them that she didn't have a black cat and told them it had to be a spirit.

Marge told me that she was very sorry that she sold that old house in Westwood because she loved living there and she never felt lonely knowing that the spirits were in the house with her. She would buy another haunted house again in a second.

My second experience in a "haunted house" was in Bergen County, New Jersey. I met the Smith's at a party where one of my established clients introduced them to me. They had just moved into an old Tudor home, and had been looking for a decorator. May had hired me to decorate the first floor so I never went upstairs, until one day when she asked if I would like to see the rest of the house. The second floor had some bedrooms and then she took me up to see the third floor.

The rooms on this level were just being used for storage. There was a room that I thought was extremely unusual! When we went to enter this room, we opened a door and about four inches from the first door was a second door. After opening the second door we found a room with a chair in the center.

The chair and the walls looked as though someone ripped them apart. The room was only about 5x5 with a very low ceiling and to me very spooky. The rocking chair that was in this room was located just above May's Master Bedroom. She said on two occasions when her husband was out, she heard the chair rocking in the night.

Let me tell you, I loved this girl. We have become very good friends but I don't think I could have lived in that house after hearing that story. I told her to throw the rocking chair away.

About six months later, they invited my family and I to dinner. While we were having dinner, we heard a toilet flush. Everyone was at the table with us so we couldn't imagine who flushed. May told us that this happened every once in a while and that sometimes she felt like someone was in the room with her. My son, who was fourteen years old at the time, had to use the bathroom but decided to wait until we returned home.

May spoke to some of the older neighbors and tried to do some research on the house. Her neighbor had some photos of the people who originally had lived in the house about 100 years before. The people were very wealthy and had a sick child who lived in the house. No one knew whether she died in the house.

I worked in this house about 21 years ago. Recently, May called me because her Mom needed help up at her new house. May, her husband Jim and their children love their home. It is really lovely now that it is decorated. My husband and I were there for dinner a few weeks ago. Everything looked great. There were no more flushing toilets and no rocking chairs. We had a wonderful evening with our friends and the best dinner I have eaten in a long time. I felt fine in the house although they told us that their next-door neighbors had some problems with their house and they think it haunted. The original people that owned May's house owned the neighbor's home too. Very strange.

"Everyone wants to hang out in my kitchen."

Don't shoot I'm the Decorator

Several years ago I decorated a beautiful home in Saddle River, New Jersey. This home was one of the loveliest homes I worked in. The entrance hall was about 1000 square feet with soft pink marble, a circular floating staircase facing a veranda, soft blush walls and mint trim. It was breathtaking.

The owners of this home were rarely there. As a matter of fact, when I arrived each morning, I would check to see if anyone had used the stove. These people had been living in the house for about a year and a half and I swear, no one ever cooked.

The only rooms they ever used were the bedroom and the gym. Because they worked and traveled so often, I had the code for the alarm system. I would go in every morning, do my work and leave.

One day I arrived at the house, entered the right number, got as far as the kitchen, and the alarm went off. I tried to disarm it but nothing I did worked. I decided to call the homeowner's office but the secretary told me that they had gone on vacation and forgot to notify me. She told me to talk to Rick, their son, who would be able to tell me what to do.

Rick got on the phone and in a very serious tone, told me to run to the front door of the house and open the front door. He said that the police would be there in a couple of minutes and if I didn't get there first they might think I was breaking in.

I didn't realize the police station was only one block away. By the time I reached the front door and opened it, the police were already there. I couldn't believe my eyes. There were two police cars and four policemen. They had their guns drawn. I was afraid that they were going to shoot me.

There I was standing in the front hallway of this magnificent house in my full-length mink coat, arms raised in the air, yelling "Please Don't shoot, I'm the decorator!" They looked at me not knowing if they should shoot or laugh.

I laugh about it now, but I have to tell you I was scared to death. I was also extremely embarrassed when I opened the newspaper the next day to read, Saddle River Police Almost Shot The Decorator. They mentioned my name and my business name. I really felt stupid! But, I must admit, it was a great way to advertise.

THE TELEPHONE CALL

It's been many years since I received a call from a woman who told me that for over a year, she and her husband had intended to call me to redecorate their home but just never got around to it. She said that she was recently widowed and she and her children were very depressed since the husband's death, especially her teen-aged daughter. Friends had suggested they redo the house. Perhaps it would give them all a lift. So she called me.

We made an appointment for a meeting at her home, and when I met her, I was impressed with her good looks. Maggie was in her early fifties, tall and slender with long blonde hair. She seemed to be very warm, kind person, even though it was clear that she was still very depressed from her loss.

As she showed me the house, we decided on a completely new look. No more humdrum Colonial that she'd been living with for years. Instead, she wanted to go contemporary, with a light, airy feeling. Both she and her daughter, Jane seemed very excited with the changes they were about to make.

Because Maggie owned and operated her own business, she would not have the time to go into the showrooms with me. Instead, I offered to bring pictures and fabric samples to the house. I invited Jane along to the showrooms to see possible furniture selections. The poor child was so sad about losing her Dad; I couldn't help but feel sorry for her. She seemed lost, but was thrilled when I asked her to come along. Maggie was grateful for my offer to her daughter.

Jane was a really sweet kid who had just started high school. She told me about some of her friends and talked about the relationship with her mom and dad and her older brother. She was a little angel whom her father adored and the sudden death at the kitchen table of this seemingly healthy man devastated her. She missed him terribly.

Our first trip into the city together was a great success. Jane couldn't believe she was actually in a New York City showroom helping to pick fabric samples and pictures of furniture for her mom. We had a late lunch together, and before we had finished our Cokes, Jane decided decorating was so much fun, maybe she would be a decorator some day.

Between the three of us, we decided on a sofa and two chairs in off-white, off-white carpeting and lovely batiste drapes. This would give us the nice, neat, monochromatic look we wanted to make the house look brighter and larger. Maggie and Jane were cheered up just thinking about the changes we would make. It seemed to be the diversion they both needed.

Orders were placed, a little construction work was done, and before long, the new furniture was delivered. Maggie called to say they were thrilled with all of our choices and could I bring over some pictures of cocktail tables. We made a date and a few evenings later, I went over with my pictures of cocktail tables of various sizes and shapes.

When I arrived at their home, a man named Morris was seated with Maggie and Jane. No sooner had I greeted Jane than she left us, "to do the dishes." Maggie invited me to sit between her and Morris so we could go over the pictures. I had noticed that Jane looked unhappy as she left us for the kitchen and I suggested that she would probably like to look at the pictures with us. But Morris insisted that Jane had to do the dishes.

I had no idea who Morris was and it was none of my business, but he didn't seem very nice. He made it clear that he didn't like any of the pictures that I brought. In fact, completely ignoring me, he told Maggie that he thought all of the tables were ugly and if she ordered any one of them, he wouldn't move in with her.

I excused myself and went to the kitchen to tell Jane good night. She looked like she was ready to cry any minute. I didn't know what to say to her, so I gave her a good night hug and told her I hoped I would see her soon. I knew something strange was going on, but I also knew it was none of my business. After all, I was only the decorator.

It was another couple of weeks before Maggie called me to say she was no longer interested in buying a table. She explained that Morris was her accountant and he had been very good to her since her husband passed away, taking her out to dinner and generally entertaining her.

Morris and Jane didn't get along. He believed this was Jane's fault because Jane was a very spoiled child. He felt she should be helping with the housekeeping after school instead of just doing her homework or being with friends

And Morris had decided that I should go to his apartment and see if any of his furniture would work with the things Maggie had bought. Because Morris seemed pretty strange, I asked my husband to come along with me. And I'm glad I did.

Morris had all sorts of weird things in his place; chairs of odd sizes and shapes and over-stuffed furniture, and on the ceiling there were wall to wall, old and junky light fixtures. I didn't want to insult him, but I didn't see one thing Maggie or anyone else, for that matter, could use.

On our way home, my husband told me that he thought Morris was a sicko and to be sure not to return to his apartment no matter what.

When I called to tell Maggie that Morris had nothing of use to her in the place, I was terribly tempted to tell her my feelings about this weird man, but I didn't want to upset her. Lucky for me that I bit my tongue, because that's when she told me she was thinking of marrying him. She sounded uncomfortable when she said he didn't think she should continue working with me. In fact, he didn't want her to spend any more money on furniture.

I found myself feeling sorry for Maggie as I wished her happiness and told her to feel free to call if she decided that she needed any more help with decorating. I asked her to give my love to Jane. Poor Jane!

About a year had gone by and I hadn't heard from Maggie and then one evening as we were in the middle of having dinner, the telephone rang. My husband answered and I heard him say. "Who is this? Are you OK?" He turned to hand me the telephone, "Someone is on the phone and she's crying."

When I heard the voice I realized it was Maggie. She was crying hysterically and talking fast. "I'm all alone, my children disowned me and I think I'm going nuts! I couldn't think of anyone else to call except you Roseann. You were always kind to Jane and myself." And then she dropped the bombshell.

"I'm going to kill myself. I'm going to commit suicide."

I gasped, but tried to keep my composure. I tried to keep her talking as I wrote a note to my husband to call the police and gave him her address. I kept listening to Maggie as she continued to talk. My heart was breaking for her.

First she lost her husband, then her children and now this. How horrible! She went on to say, "Morris says that I'm crazy and that I should be dead. He's so abusive to me. Things have gotten so bad between Jane and Morris that she had to move in with her brother. Everything is so miserable. I don't want to live any more."

"My family and friends don't talk to me. Morris is so abusive. He hits me and calls me names and tells me how stupid I am. I don't know who to turn to. I think I would be better off dead. Please tell Jane I love her so much," and then there was silence, she hung up.

My heart was pounding. I didn't know what to do. I grabbed my coat and car keys and I found myself driving to Maggie's house. By the time I arrived, I saw two police cars and an ambulance. Maggie had already slit her wrists. It was a dreadful sight. She was laying on the bathroom floor unconscious in a pool of blood. They got her to the hospital on time to save her. Thank God!

I tried to get information about Maggie but because I was not an immediate member of the family they wouldn't talk to me. I heard a few stories but never could find out what happened to Maggie, Jane or Morris.

About two years later, as I sat in the Westwood dinner having lunch, a pretty woman walked over to my table. At first I didn't recognize her and then I realized it was Maggie. She looked a little thinner, a little older but for what she had gone through, Maggie looked well.

She asked if she could sit down to talk to me. "I dialed your number so many times Roseann. I wanted to talk to you and thank you for helping me on that dreadful night but I kept hanging up because I was so embarrassed to talk to you. If you hadn't kept me on the telephone talking that night I would probably be dead. I really didn't want to live. I'm so happy that I saw you sitting here today."

Maggie continued talking with tears in her eyes. "After I was hospitalized the police started questioning me and they started investigating Morris. A woman had called me that same day. The day I tried to commit suicide. She said that I shouldn't trust Morris. She said he was a fraud and he was only there for the money. She told me to call the police because she knew Morris had something to do with my husband's death."

"It was so horrible and I was so mixed up, I felt that I couldn't go on any more. She told me that it wasn't the first time that Morris tried something like this but he always got away with it."

"I did a really stupid thing and I confronted Morris about what this woman told me. At first he denied it and then when I said I was going to the police, he told me if I went to the police he would say that I had something to do with it and we would both go to jail. This is when I felt so helpless. I didn't know what to do."

Maggie told me that the police investigated and they exhumed her husband's body and found out that Morris had been poisoning him and did indeed kill him. Whatever he was using to poison her husband made it look like he had a heart attack.

Morris is in prison now. Maggie is still alone. Her children did not forgive her, although they are all going for counseling together. Maggie kept talking and I kept listening. I was so sad for all of them but I was happy that I was there for her. She was determined to win the children back. She said she was trying to put her life back together.

Again, Maggie thanked me, gave me a big hug and told me she would never forget what I did for her. I was speechless. I realized I hadn't said a word to her for the whole time she was at the table. She did all the talking. After Maggie left, I sat at the table and cried and thanked God that she called me that night.

I never heard from Maggie again. I think of her often, and pray for her all the time. I do hope she reunites with Jane because even though she made a lot of mistakes, they really need one another.

HE SAID HE DIDN'T KNOW ME

Over the years country clubs have become very popular in Bergen and Rockland Counties. I have been called in to work on several of them.

About five years ago, I was asked to do some work in a country club in Rockland County. They said on the telephone they wanted to redo a woman's and men's locker room. I had never decorated a locker room before, but there's a first time for everything. The following Saturday I met with the president of the club along with three ladies who were selected to be the decorating committee.

First we looked at the women's locker room, which had orange cinder block walls and a cement floor. It looked like everyone's unfinished basement only they painted the blocks orange. After discussing some possibilities, we moved along to the men's locker room. The president offered to look in the showers before I entered in case any men were showering. When he came out, he told me the coast was clear.

When I entered the locker, a man in about his late sixties suddenly came out from a shower stall. He was completely naked and was shocked to see a man and three other women standing there looking at his nakedness. I wasn't actually looking at his body, but as I looked at his shocked face, I thought I recognized him.

The next thing I heard come from my mouth was "You look so familiar! Where do I know you from?"

He looked at me totally humiliated and said "I don't know you lady. I have never seen you before in my life. What the hell are you doing here and what the hell are you talking about?" He then ran to hide in the stall and grabbed a towel to cover up.

It wasn't until everyone started laughing that I realized what I had said "You look so familiar" is not what you say to a naked person. The poor old man did recognize me but was too embarrassed to admit it.

He met me while I was doing construction on a new house in his neighborhood. He had stopped by to see how the house was coming along and had talked to me.

I heard sometime later, he was quite the ladies' man and he had a reputation with the women. When I started working at the club, he avoided me like the plague. He never looked me in the face, and I made sure I only looked at his face!

I learned a very valuable lesson; I will never tell another person that he or she looks familiar either with or without their clothes on.

"Create your home so it becomes your own."

OUR FATHER WHO ART IN HEAVEN

My three children attended Catholic grammar school in Westwood, New Jersey. The school was originally run by the Sisters Of Charity from Convent Station, New Jersey but when my children attended the school we only had two nuns.

When my son Scott was about ten years old, the Pope was visiting the United States and Sister Claire took his class over to the convent so the children could watch the Pope on television. It wasn't like today with televisions in every classroom.

This was the first time that Scott was in a convent and he was shocked to see how badly the sisters lived. Throughout the place was chipped paint; the walls had holes so you could actually look into the next room. The convent was a total mess. The furniture was all second hand. Nothing matched and this really upset Scott.

He decided that because I was a decorator I should buy these two nuns all new furniture and that I should redecorate for them. He just didn't have any conception at ten years old, that it takes money to buy furniture and decorate. For some reason, Scott thought I should do it.

I tried to explain to him that I would be happy to help the sisters, but they would need some money to do the work. Scott was very stubborn, when he got something in his head he wouldn't give up until he got it done.

The next thing I knew I got a telephone call from Sister Claire. "Hi Mrs. Kearney this is Sister Claire from St. Andrews School. Your son, Scott told me that you are a decorator and that you would like to help us fix up the convent." I was going to kill him when he came home.

My children had just started going to this school and I hadn't had the pleasure of meeting Sister Claire and I didn't want to make a bad impression, but I knew what I was in for.

She went on to ask me if I would meet with her and the other sister to sit and talk. Scott had volunteered my services and I knew I was in trouble.

The following day, I met with Sister Claire and Sister Roberta and they took me around the old building. Scott wasn't exaggerating, it was really a mess and it was sad that in this day and age, these two women were living in this building that should have been condemned by the Board of Health.

I am also a softy, so when I saw all of this I knew I had to do something to help. But I knew it would cost money to renovate the place.

I had noticed a charming brick building, a two-story colonial right next door between the old convent and the rectory a couple of doors away from the church. I asked how long the building had been empty and who owned it. Sister told me that it was owned by the parish and that no one had lived there for years. I had an idea! The house looked like it was in great condition from the outside. Maybe the church would let us use it for the convent. If the interior looked as good as the exterior it wouldn't be hard to fix it up and make it livable for these sisters who did so much for our children.

Sister Claire asked me if I would talk to the pastor, Father Driscole. She said that she didn't get along very well with him and that it would be a good idea if I did the talking. She said that he was a grumpy old priest. She really had her doubts that Father would even listen to me and our proposal but as it turned out, she was dead wrong.

I made an appointment with Father Driscole. I expected to meet a terrible old grouch, who wouldn't give me the time of day. Instead, I met with a delightful, sweet, little old man who I feel in love with. He couldn't have been nicer. I found out later that Sister Claire and Father Driscole didn't get along because he was an old-school priest and Sister Claire was unconventional, to say the least.

She didn't wear a habit, which Father Driscole thought was terrible. Sister smoked and sometimes, she drank too. Father thought this was not the way a sister should behave. I have to admit, I agreed with him that these were not the normal actions of a nun. At least, not the nuns I once knew. You just don't think of a nun smoking.

Sister Claire truly had a few strange habits and I don't mean the kind you wear. Good old Father Driscole seemed to be willing to let us use the building as the convent as long as I was the mediator, so he didn't have to deal with Sister Claire.

Well it was a start. There were several meetings with Sister Claire, Father Driscole and a committee we put together to work on this project.

Father Driscole was willing to take up one collection in church for the renovations on the building but that was all. He didn't think it was fair to the poor people in the parish to have to pay for something like that. "People have their own problems," he said.

We took up a collection and made $1300.00, not much but it went far. We never asked the parishioners for another cent. Some people in the parish donated things to the house, gifts that they gave because they loved the sisters.

It was amazing how many people got involved. One group of parishioners got together to form the painting committee. One of the parishioners arranged to have his employer donate all the paint that we needed. We found a man in the parish who was a carpenter and another, that was a plumber and so on and we got the job done.

People donated old fireplace screens and andirons and all kinds of other things and I fixed them up and put as much to use as I could. I also went to some of my showrooms for donations, of furniture and carpets and finally, when the work was done, it was beautiful.

Some of the people were a little shocked by what they saw. They expected everything to be black and white because it was a convent and of course, it wasn't anything like that. The color scheme was mauve and gray. One of the men who was painting, Ed Murtugh, thought we had purchased the wrong paint. When he opened the first can he stopped everyone from painting. Although he was shocked at the start, he loved it when it was completed and so did the sisters.

We decided to have an Open House for the parish so everyone could view what we had done as a team. The sisters were thrilled because they had a nice new house and Father Driscole was so happy because he didn't have to spend a cent but we had made major improvements on his building.

Father was great about the whole thing. Instead of the little old priest I saw in church, he was young at heart and full of fun and always had a joke to tell.

He became a great friend and member of my family. Father Driscole had to leave the parish a couple of years after the convent was restored because the Archdiocese said he was not a good administrator. It didn't make a difference that he was the best damn priest around, who cared about the people, his parish and his community.

When he was asked to leave, he didn't have a place to stay. He was crushed. St. Andrew's had been his home for over 13 years. He loved the people in the parish. The news devastated him. He called and asked us if it were all right if he stay with us until he got settled. He ended up staying with us for about four months until he was offered a job in Washington, D.C. teaching at Catholic University and also working at the Veterans Hospital.

He would come and stay with us every holiday that he had time off. He would dance with my daughters who were 6 and 9 years old, play word games with my son, have very intellectual talks with my husband, Cyril. He really was a member of the family and always made fun of my cooking.

Father Driscole became ill while he was in Washington, D.C. but five minutes before he died, I received a telephone call from his brother Frank. Frank told me that an old friend wanted to talk to me. In a low muffled voice that I could barely hear, I heard his voice say, "Roseann, I love you." And Father Driscole went to heaven. I can't explain my loss; I only can tell you that we loved him dearly.

Father Driscole will always be a part of our lives. He was a father to me and a grandfather to my children and my son's best friend and the greatest priest I ever met. We have fond memories of him. We would have never met him if my son didn't volunteer my services as a decorator. Thank you Scott, for being so stubborn.

THE LADY IS A TRAMP

Doris was a short, portly, chubby, blond haired, perky lady who for some reason, thought she looked like Marilyn Monroe. She definitely had a very high opinion of herself but my contractors thought she looked like a munchkin from Willie Wonka and the Chocolate Factory.

One of my contractors had been working on an addition for her when Doris asked if he knew a decorator that he could recommend. He didn't know what had happened to the last decorator but knew she was no longer working with Doris. John gave her my number and she called me for a consultation. I remember the first question she asked me was if I had a lot of time to spend with her because she admitted she had a very difficult time making decisions and she needed someone who would spend time with her and someone who had patience.

I told her I could surely spend time with her as long as she understood that I got paid by the hour. I also told her it shouldn't be so difficult making the decisions that we had to make because I had been doing this for many year and I would make it easy for her. She seemed pleased and asked if I could start immediately.

Our first project was renovating a bathroom. The room was already gutted out but she had not yet ordered the marble for the floor. We went out the same day to look at marble and found something that we both liked. Doris seemed very happy and I told her that we really could make all the selections for the room over the next couple of days and as soon as the marble came, I had a great marble man to install.

I noticed that Doris was extremely demanding with the workers. Before they even started a project, she warned them that it better be perfect or they would have to redo it. She only accepted perfection. I tried to reassure her that my contractors were perfectionists, and not to worry.

After I had been working there a few weeks my contractors started telling me things that I wasn't quite sure how to handle. A few of the guys said that she purposely would rub against them, and that she was always flirting and saying things to them that they felt were inappropriate.

One day shortly after my contractors spoke to me about this. Doris and I were on one of our shopping expeditions. She began to talk to me about how good-looking she thought one of the salesmen was. She then decided to tell me that Sam, the man she was living with and the man I thought was her husband was not her husband. She said they had been living together for the past thirteen years. He was supposed to marry her after she got divorced but his attorney stopped the marriage.

Sam was very wealthy and his attorney felt that it was not a wise move for him to remarry at that time. At least this is what she told me. She told me that the reason she stayed with him was his money. She outwardly admitted that she took as much from him as she possibly could. Her 19-year-old daughter also lived in the house with them. Sam bought her horses, clothes and expensive sport cars. Doris and her daughter spent his money like it was water.

Doris told me that she would have an affair if the right person came along and that she was anxious to find someone because she was lonely and horny. I was shocked at the things that she was telling me. I only knew her for a couple of weeks.

I realized that my men weren't joking and that she was hitting on them. I knew my contractors very well so I met with them and had a long talk about the situation. They weren't at all shocked because she had already made a pass at almost all of them. They all found it funny because none of them thought she was the least bit attractive and thought she was obnoxious.

As my workers continued to refuse her advances one by one she began to get nastier and nastier. She was never pleased with anyone or anything. The guys were getting more and more unhappy and each day we began to have more problems. This never happened to us before. My contractors go to work every morning. They get there on time, they work a full day, they work hard, and they get paid and move on to the next client.

I tried to talk to her without insulting her but I couldn't reason with her. I told the guys to try to work in twos and to try to finish up quickly. As time went by she became more and more demanding with me. It was Christmas time and when she heard that I have a Christmas tree in every room in my home she told me that's what she wanted. I couldn't understand this, because I knew she was Jewish, but I gave her what she wanted.

The only problem was she expected me to be there more and more hours and I didn't have time for my other clients. I was getting to work at 7:30 AM every morning and leaving her house at night at 7:00 PM. On a couple of occasions she asked me to go out to dinner with her. I went once but after that I told her I had to get home to my family. On a few occasions she suggested that I sleep over because it was snowing and she was afraid I would get into an accident. Again, I refused and told her I had a family at home.

I started working for her the previous May and during the year she had given me unexpected gifts. Easter she had given me flowers and candy. Valentines day she gave me a beautiful address book. Christmas she gave me a very expensive Coach briefcase and she also sent gifts to my family and notes thanking them for sharing their mother with her.

Right after Christmas she went on vacation and she would call me sometimes 2 or 3 times a day telling me that she missed me and couldn't wait until she got back. In April she had invited me to go away to a spa with her. The reason for this was because she said she felt so guilty because she had been working me so hard. Again I refused and she became very upset. I really didn't know why she was so mad at me.

The following week when she returned from the spa I went back to the house to finish my work. I walked into the house very early one morning. Everything seemed quiet. I thought maybe she decided to stay at the spa for a few extra days. I was happy about this because we were hoping to finish up and get out of there. We had clients who had been waiting for us for a very long time. I called out her name and no one answered. As I walked closer to her bedroom, I suddenly heard talking and laughing. I thought maybe she was on the telephone. I knocked on the door and she told me to come in.

When I entered the room, I noticed all the shades were pulled down and when I looked over at the bed, I saw that Doris was in bed with a woman. She boldly introduced me to this woman as her new decorator and she told me in a very loud, nasty tone "Roseann, this could have been you". I was stunned and speechless. I couldn't believe my eyes or my ears.

She was still talking and shouting as I was walking towards the front door. She was demanding that I not leave. She threatened that if I left she would sue me for not completing the job. I told her to sue me. "You have a new decorator that means you released me of my duties. Let her finish the job. Take me to court". She actually tried to take me to court but she didn't have a leg to stand on and I guess she realized it because I stopped getting calls from her. She owed me some money, but I really didn't care and neither did my contractors we were just so happy to be out of there. This lady is a tramp!

*"The porch wraps around the back of the house. A touch of
Victorian and a touch of the tropics"*

My LITTLE PRINCESS

She was 23 years old with long, silky blond hair and big blue eyes. I knew the minute I set eyes on her that she was a sweet person and I was going to like her.

It was about 7 years ago when we met. Skyler called me for a consultation. She and her fiancé had just bought a lovely townhouse in Goshen, New York. They needed help decorating and she called me. Skyler told me that she knew what she wanted. At least, she knew what color she wanted to paint. PINK! Not a bright, candy pink, but a soft blush colored pink. A pink that truly reminded me of Skyler.

The first question I asked her was if her fiancé liked the color pink. Did you discuss this with him?" "Yes, of course I did she replied". Mario said it was fine. I could do anything I want to when it comes to decorating the house. (Mario, I thought, pink just doesn't sound like a Mario color!).

Mario sounded like a peach of a guy so we continued making plans for the house. We took a few trips into the city and ordered furniture, pink, of course. Even the wood on the dining room table was pickled pink, but it honestly looked beautiful when it was completed. Skyler really did have good taste. She selected nice pieces. We added some hand painted pieces, a miniature grandfather clock in the entrance hall and lots of great accessories. Money didn't seem to be an issue. Skyler bought anything that she wanted and just kept writing out checks.

I told. Jack and Ken, the painters who were working on this assignment for me, that they could start painting. On the third day that they were there, I received a frantic telephone call from Jack. "Roseann, a real tough guy came in and said his name was Mario Letuccia. Do you know who he is? The family owns the largest sanitation company in New Jersey. They are all involved in organized crime. You know, the Mafia. He told us to stop painting and to get the hell out."

Jack honestly didn't care what the guy did for a living but he said that he was afraid of this guy. "He told us he wasn't going to live in a FUCKIN PINK HOUSE and to get the hell out before he killed us."

Jack was calling from a telephone booth and he didn't know what to do. I took his telephone number and told him that I would try to reach Skyler and I would call him right back. I called Skyler and told her what had happened and she thought it was quite funny. She told me to tell the painter to go back." "You must be kidding, you are crazy they are scared to death of Mario". She told me she would call Mario and than they could return.

Skyler called the men and they did continue to paint pink. She reassured Mario that the house was going to be beautiful and that he would love it when it was done. She told him, please just trust me and leave the painters alone. He said okay and he calmed down.

The furniture was delivered and the townhouse was stunning. Mario loved it so much he wanted me to have it published in a decorating magazine.

I continued working with Skyler and Mario and than she asked me if I would help coordinate her wedding. Her mom worked and didn't know much about wedding planning and she wanted the wedding to be perfect.

We found a charming place to hold the reception in Long Island where Skyler grew up. It was a country club right on the water and it was breathtaking. Skyler wanted this wedding to be her way, beautiful, elegant with a touch of country and if I had to guess, PINK! We decided this would be the place.

We then designed gowns for the bridal party and a gown for Skyler. We selected china, glassware, tablecloths and flowers and the cake. We made arrangements at the church and were ready. At this point, I had gotten so close to Skyler that I felt like one of my own daughters, was getting married.

Skyler and Mario were having a dress rehearsal on Friday. She asked me to please come to the rehearsal because she needed me to coordinate the procession in church. She also wanted me to be at the rehearsal dinner on Friday evening. She was so nervous and didn't think she would get through it without me. Skyler and I had become extremely close, not just as a designer, client relationship, she became one of my kids and I loved her. We talked about everything. She always asked me for my advice and I loved helping her in anyway that I could.

My husband and I went out Friday evening for the rehearsal and then the dinner. It was a super weekend. Skyler had made reservations for us to stay as her guests in a wonderful little Inn right on the water. It was lovely.

Saturday morning came so quickly and the day was finally here. I called Skyler to see how she was doing and she sounded fine but told me to make sure I get over to her mom's house to make sure she looked all right. I thought, "How could she not look all right?" She was so beautiful and I was sure she was going to be the most magnificent bride that I had ever seen. I didn't have any doubts and I was right. When I walked into her mom's house and saw her standing there in her wedding gown, I couldn't believe my eyes. She looked like a princess. Her gown was breathtaking. It was made of pure white silk with fine French lace and beading, her hair was up with soft, silky tendrils hanging down the side of her sweet face. She was perfect.

I followed her limo over to the church in the limo that she provided for us. In the back of the church I fixed her gown and veil and got her ready to walk down the isle to meet her prince.

I sat in a pew with my husband and watched My Little Princess walk down the isle to the wedding march. My eyes were filled with tears. I knew how it would feel when it was time to give one of my children away to someone else. I knew just how it would feel when one of my children would get married. This girl, this beautiful stranger became such a big part of my life. She truly became a part of me.

The reception was great and the wedding was over; Skyler and Mario went on their honeymoon. A few days after they left, I received a telephone call from them thanking me for all of my help. They told me they would have never been able to do it without me. They said that they would see me when they came home. They were wonderful kids.

Since than I have been called to decorate several other homes for them. Skyler called me to decorate a baby nursery for their baby who was now about two years old. She is now pregnant with her second baby and I'm sure I will be doing something special for this new addition too.

I have been working in this business for many years. I have met many wonderful people and some strange ones but it is rare that you find someone like Skyler. Last October, I was rushed to the hospital with a massive GI hemorrhage. I was very sick and in intensive care for about four weeks.

My three children were at my bedside each and every day along with my fourth child Skyler. Skyler came to the hospital everyday. She did what every good daughter would do for her mother. I had to have blood transfusions and very difficult procedures and when they wheeled me out of the room, there stood Skyler, along with my children. She waited for me, making sure that I was alright, kissing my face and holding my hand and reassuring me that everything would be ok. Mario, the tough guy, even called me at the hospital to see if I needed anything, to tell me not to worry about anything, and he told me he loved me.

Skyler and I just went to lunch today. She was in town to see her doctor and called and asked me out to lunch. She is now about 6 months pregnant and as beautiful or more beautiful than ever. I looked across the table at her today and I knew how lucky I was that she had called me for that consultation. I don't know how we became so close but we did. It must have been fate. I know Skyler will always be a part of my life and she will always be My Little Princess!

PERSONAL ADS

I've been in business for quite a few years and I've never advertised. All of my clients are referred to me by previous clients. Usually a person sees work that I have done and they call me. This is exactly what happened with my client in Hackensack.

I received a call from Lucy who lived in a very big, old house. Lucy told me that she had just moved into this house about four months earlier, and she and her husband had great plans for this magnificent house. She went on to tell me that since her and her husband bought the house, they had separated and so her dreams of doing a lot of work were now slim. "I would still like to do some work and make some changes, but I know I can't do as much as we expected to do."

She then made an appointment to meet with me for a consultation and I looked forward to meeting with her.

It was Wednesday morning, a very sunny, cheerful day in October when I first met Lucy. Lucy was a 42-year-old woman. She wore too much make-up. She had very bleached blonde hair and after talking to her for a few minutes, I got the impression that she was a little flaky.

You must understand, FLAKY, is not unusual in my business. Lucy went on to tell me that she loved Art Deco design and that she would like to turn this lovely old traditional home into something with lots of ART DECO decorations. I was a little heart broken because this big old house had so much charms and style just the way it was. I agreed, the house needed to be worked on but not changed so drastically. I asked her if she were sure and we discussed some other possibilities, but there was no changing her mind. Lucy decided to paint the whole house in all pastels and we made a second appointment to go to the city on the following Monday morning to look at furniture.

I arrived at her house about nine o'clock the following Monday morning as we had arranged. I rang the doorbell several times but no one answered the door. A couple of minutes later, a woman who was about sixty years old came to the front door and ushered me into Lucy's parlor. "Come in," she said, "Miss Lucy will be down shortly."

I waited in this room for about forty-five minutes and than got up to find the housekeeper. "Excuse me," I said, "is everything alright, I have been waiting for about forty five minutes and Lucy never came down. Is something wrong?"

The woman went on to tell me that Miss Lucy wasn't feeling well and again said she would be down shortly. I expressed my concern and told her that if Lucy wasn't feeling well, we could change the day of our appointment. But the woman persisted that

Miss Lucy would be right down.

About fifteen minutes later I heard talking in the hall and it was Lucy and the housekeeper. I walked out into the hallway and saw Lucy at the top of the staircase. She was dressed in bright yellow pedal pushers. Her pants were very tight. She had on a bright red sweater, which was also very tight, and very revealing and very high-heeled shoes. Along with her bright bleached hair and red lipstick, she was quite a sight!

As I watched in disbelief, Lucy moved like she was in extreme pain. It was quite evident that she was having difficulty walking. As she not so gracefully tried to walk down the stairs, I asked her if she would like to cancel this appointment and reschedule for another day. Lucy assured me that she was fine and went on to tell me that since her husband left her, she had been answering personal ads.

Lucy continued talking but from the moment that I heard personal ads, I tried to block everything out. This very strange lady that I didn't know, was telling me about the date that she had with a complete stranger and was telling me about the sex that she had with this stranger. Oh my god! I really didn't want to hear anything else but I couldn't stop her from talking. I was probably standing in the middle of the entrance hall with my mouth wide open in shock that she would be telling me these things.

I told her that if she didn't feel well we could skip this appointment. I just didn't want to hear about her positions! I thought, I'm going to have to listen to this all day long.

I really didn't want to hear her stories and to tell you the truth, when I took a good look at her I honestly didn't want to take her into

New York City showrooms dressed the way she was. Yes it was October, but it wasn't Halloween!

There was no way to get out of this one. Lucy wanted to go to New York and I swore that when I got my hands on the person that referred her to me, I would strangle them.

As soon as we got into the car, I turned the radio on. I was hoping that if she heard the music maybe she would stop talking. This technique did not work. She talked above the music and by hook or by crook she was going to tell me stories even though I didn't want to hear them.

All I could think of was, "Is nothing sacred?" Lucy told me that she had been answering the personal ads since her husband left her. She had been married for about nineteen years and all of her friends were married. She decided this was the only way to meet men. I tried to change the subject to decorating, but she just kept talking about her crazy adventures.

She met and dated a man who was handicapped. He had lost his legs in the Viet Nam War. She felt sorry for him when she spoke to him on the telephone so she agreed to go out on a date with him and of course, they ended up in bed. Lucy thought he was the best because he could do things other men couldn't do. I was truly getting sick to my stomach and I didn't want to hear anything else.

I quickly changed the subject onto my very bad headache and told her I thought I had a sinus infection and I was going to make an appointment with the doctor when we returned home. This was another big mistake because than she went on to tell me about the doctor that she was seeing in the city. She met this one at a party and found him so extremely attractive that even though nothing was wrong with her physically, she made an appointment to see him at his office. She made sure to buy very sexy undergarments because she knew that she could turn him on. The poor doctor, didn't have a chance.

We finally reached the showroom and she finally stopped talking. Whenever we entered a showroom, all eyes were on us. A few of the people that I worked with regularly asked me without Lucy hearing, "Where did you pick her up?" Of course, I didn't answer but I was thinking the same thing.

It was very interested working with Lucy. She always had a new story to tell me, if I wanted to hear it or not.

We never got to finish decorating her house. She ordered furniture, but she sold the house before the furniture was delivered. I heard she did go back with her husband for a while but they are now officially divorced. I often think of Lucy and wonder how these crazy but very real people happen to find me.

Not too long ago, I met Lucy at a party given by one of my clients. As soon as Lucy saw me, she ran over to me and started telling me more crazy stories about the new loves in her life. Yes, I said loves. She's back to answering the personal ads!

*"Who needs to go on vacation. This is my very own
Shangri-La"*

KNOCKED UP!

Usually, baby nurseries are so much fun to decorate, as I said, usually.

I was working in a house in Avalon, New Jersey. I was decorating a nursery for a woman who was expecting twins.

Jamie was confined to bed on a monitor because she had been having contractions early in her pregnancy and the doctor didn't want to take any unnecessary chances. He ordered complete bed rest.

Every morning when I arrived at work, I went into Jamie's room and either brought her a little breakfast or a book or something to cheer her up. It's hard staying in bed for nine months. It becomes very boring.

On several occasions Jamie had to be taken to the hospital. The contractions had gotten so bad, but would always stop when she got to the hospital. The doctors would send her home. It was always a false alarm.

One day, while we were working in the nursery, we heard moaning coming from the master bedroom. I ran into her room and Jamie was having bad contractions again. We waited a few minutes but they continued so we called her husband Todd who worked close by and he said he would come right home to take her to the hospital.

As I was helping Jamie get ready I heard unusual sounds coming from the nursery. When I went to see what was happening, I found my artist, Joe, on the floor, holding his stomach and moaning. "Stop fooling around," I said. This isn't funny. I'm trying to get Jamie ready to go to the hospital. Joe stayed on the floor and moaned in pain. He wasn't kidding. He said he didn't know what was wrong. He had felt OK and than suddenly he began to get sharp stomach pains. "I can't even stand up the pain is so bad," said Joe".

I decided not to wait for Todd and I called 911 for an ambulance. I was afraid I couldn't handle both of them and I wanted to get them to the hospital quickly.

I heard Todd's car pull into the garage and right behind him followed an ambulance. Todd didn't know what was happening. He heard Jamie crying in one room and Joe moaning in the other. I quickly tried to explain what was going on.

The ambulance took both Jamie and Joe to the hospital. Todd asked me to stay at the house with the Nanny and his two year old. He promised me that he would call me as soon as he had any information about either of them.

I was pacing the floor and finally 2 hours later the telephone rang and Todd told me that Jamie was in labor and that Joe was going into surgery. He said that Joe had to have emergency surgery. When I asked him why, he started to laugh. "Roseann, you won't believe it. Joe got knocked up!" I started laughing and asked what was really wrong with him. Todd persisted, "Roseann, I'm not kidding it's true. He's really knocked up".

The doctor said that when Joe was in his mother's womb, he was supposed to be a twin. The egg somehow split and ended up inside Joe. He had been carrying this embryo since he was born, no one ever noticed it on an x-ray and finally today it ruptured. Joe is very lucky he got to the hospital so quickly. The doctor told me that this is very rare. They did hear of several other cases that were similar but not here in the US. Of course, it would happen to one of my subs on a nursery job. The doctor also said that his pain was very severe like a woman in labor.

We were happy to hear that Joe came through the surgery with flying colors and Jamie gave birth ten hours later to two beautiful baby girls Trish and Laurel.

I was happy that Joe had finished painting the nursery that day before he and Jamie went into labor.

Trish and Laurel are very happy in their lovely pink and white faux hand painted room with clouds on the ceiling, white cribs and hand painted armoire. The window treatments were in a beautiful flowered white and pink chintz fabric almost as pretty and sweet as the twins. I said almost.

All are doing well. Jamie and Joe both had c-sections and recuperated just fine!

$\mathscr{S}$LEEP WALKING

Building bookcases isn't a difficult job but when you hear heavy breathing right behind you, you want to finish quickly and get out.

This is what happened to one of my general contractors, Mike. I sent him to a client named Camilla in Bergen who lived in a townhouse. Mike was building bookcases on either side of the client's fireplace when he heard heavy breathing right behind him. He turned to take a look and saw this 300-pound female client lying on the floor all curled up in a ball fast asleep. He didn't know exactly what to do, stopped for a second and thought, "should I wake her?" No, she must have wanted to lie on the floor. I know she didn't pass out, I would have heard her fall. He never even heard her come into the room. He probably didn't hear anything because he works with his radio blasting and he was also hammering. She never said anything to him but this was very strange.

Mike decided to keep working. "If I keep hammering, maybe, she will wake up". She lay there fast asleep, almost comatose. He finished building the bookcases, very carefully cleaned up, climbed over her and left.

When he got home, of course, he called me and told me what happened. I said if I had the opportunity, I would say something to her, but as long as he was finished with the job, I told him not to worry about it.

A couple of days later, I got a call from my painter, Jack who said that he and Ken were painting and the same exact thing happened to them. Only, they saw her come in, put a pillow on the floor and lay down.

Jack didn't know what to do, and having a completely different personality than Mike, he and Ken decided they just wanted to get the hell out of there. They didn't know what she was up to and didn't want to get accused of any wrong doings.

Of course, when I received Jack's call I knew I had to call Camilla. Before I had a chance to call her, my telephone rang. She was calling me. "I don't understand, she said. I know that Jack and Ken were at my house this morning but they didn't get anything done." "Do you know why?" "Yes Camilla." I just received a call from Jack who was very upset and I told her what Jack told me. There was dead silence; she seemed shocked. I told her how uncomfortable the guys felt and then she decided to tell me what she thought had happened. She said that she was on medication and whenever she took this medicine, it put her to sleep. She went on to say "I must have been sleepwalking!" She kept apologizing and begged me to send the painters back the next day. The following day, the painter returned, but so did I. Everything seemed fine. The guys finished almost everything and I told Camilla we would return the next day to finish.

When we went back the next morning, we found red circles all over the walls that had just been painted. Someone had drawn small red circles, with notes next to them saying, paint here. We looked at one another in disbelief and I called Camilla down from her bedroom. Camilla told us that she didn't remember doing any of this and again persisted that she must have done this while she was sleep walking.

I told Camilla that we had to finish the job that same day. People had been waiting for the painters and we really just wanted to get out. I stayed with my painters. I made sure they completed the job. We got paid and left.

A few days later, Camilla called and asked me to go back to her house to start a new project. I told her we were very busy and couldn't take on any more jobs.

I later heard that she had a breakdown and that she was on all different types of medication. I was told that after we completed her job, her condition became more serious and she ended up hospitalized.

Unfortunately, when you take a job, you never know what the people are going to be like. I'm sure she was harmless but we knew she had some kind of problem and we didn't want to get caught up in it.

HARDHATS AND ELEVATORS

It was about nine years ago when a client of mine from River Vale invited my husband and I to join them along with a group of their friends, to dinner. We had a wonderful time. We met their friends who were so much fun and very interesting.

I was seated next to a woman who had been living in Japan with her husband for the past four years. His company sent him there for a five-year stint and he was preparing to retire when his time was up. Betty told us that they were thinking of retiring in Washington, D.C. and they had also just purchased a second home in Williamsburg, Virginia when Jeff was asked to go to Japan. It sounded like they traveled all over the world and it was interesting listening to them.

While we were having dinner, Betty mentioned that she had asked Pat, my client, to invite us to come along for dinner because she wanted to meet me. She told me that she loved the work I had done at Pat's house and she asked if I would be interested in working with them in Washington, D.C. when they found a new residence. "Sure," I replied, "I would love that." I told her I would be interested and to call me when she knew what she was going to do and exactly where they were going to live.

I thought this was great but I truly didn't give it a second thought because a lot of people say they are going to call you and then they change there mind.

About six months later, while I was working in my office with another client, the telephone rang. When I answered, a very cheery woman by the name of Betty was calling me. Hi Roseann, I don't know if you remember me, its Betty Ketler from Japan.

Japan, I thought, of course, I know who it was; I don't get many calls from Japan.

Betty told me that she and her husband were retiring in May and that they had purchased a 4000 square foot condo at the Ritz Carlton on M Street, Washington, D.C. She asked if I would still be interested in decorating and designing for them.

Surprised to hear from her, but happy that she remembered to call me I immediately said yes. "I'd love to work for you and Jeff".

She went on to tell me that they were flying into Washington in a few weeks and she wanted me to meet them so I could see the condo. "If there are any structural changes you want to make this is the time to do it. We made an appointment to meet in Washington in two weeks.

Stacey, my daughter who collaborated with me on this job and I met the Ketler's in front of the Ritz as planned. Unfortunately Betty forgot to tell me that the Ritz was still under construction and the only way you could get to her apartment was on an open, outside elevator. I guess I forgot to mention that I hate elevators to begin with and the thought of going up on an open outside elevator made me sick to my stomach.

Of course, I couldn't say anything to them I would have looked like a real jerk. They handed me a hardhat as they escorted me to this rickety looking outdoor elevator. I took one look at Stacey and I knew she knew what I was feeling. We all got onto the elevator and I immediately but very properly moved to the middle and said a fast prayer.

I was really surprised that they were allowing us into the building at this time because it really was dangerous. A hard hat really wouldn't have done much for us if something fell on us or if we fell through something. I later found out that they gave the Ketler's special permission because they weren't able to go back to Washington until sometime in May when they were planning to move in. We had to make a few architectural changed now while the building was still under construction.

I made the necessary changes and I knew I was going to have to get back on that elevator again. It was the only way out.

Betty and Jeff were amazing people to work with. Every second was an adventure. Because we were decorating long distance we had to make sure all of our measurements were very accurate. We e-mailed one another often and talked on the telephone daily. The Ketler's had a second residence in Williamsburg, Virginia that we were decorating at the same time. I just loved this house. It was on the Saint James River and it was so pretty.

The Ketler's made another trip in to meet with me in December. We only had one day to shop for both homes so we really had a lot to get done.

We had a magnificent day. We shopped at a showroom that had almost every piece of furniture that we needed. We bought 57 pieces in one day. It was great. It was amazing because most clients have a hard time selecting one piece of furniture. The Ketler's were very decisive. They knew, as soon as they saw something if they liked it. Luckily, we worked wonderfully together. Everything just clicked.

At this point, we had to make decisions on who was going to do the work in Williamsburg and when. They didn't know any contractors in Virginia and again asked if they could use my contractors who they would put up in hotels. I told them that this would be costly but they didn't care, they just wanted it to get done and get done correctly. This ended up being a great experience for all of us. The Ketler's loved the contractors and tried to make them feel at home. She even made them a real southern barbeque.

It really was a tremendous amount of work because the Ketler's and I were driving back and forth to Washington from Virginia and decorating both residences at one time. Every piece of furniture was perfect. Nothing had to be returned. We worked long, hard days. We stayed in Williamsburg for two and a half weeks but we got everything done. I had 12 contractors with me.

In Washington I only had three people helping me because we didn't have construction work to do. We only had to paint and wallpaper and accessorize. My window treatment man came and measured the windows and returned to hang them when they were completed. I know it's hard to believe, but the whole experience was delightful and I would do it all over again.

We remained friends with the Ketler's. They invited us to their daughter's wedding, which was held at the Watergate Hotel in Washington. The following day, they held a brunch at their condo at the Ritz and it was lovely.

Betty just sent me an e-mail yesterday with a picture of her new grandchild. She now has four grandchildren.

My job with the Ketler's was great and the elevator ride really wasn't so bad. The good thing about the whole experience was that I overcame my fear of elevators. By going on that outdoor elevator, I realized I could do almost anything.

"Lou, my own personal Pastry Chef. Every room should have a touch of whimsy"

DESPERATE HOUSEWIVES

Most people believe that the television show Desperate Housewives is fictitious; written just to entertain us. My belief is that the writers somehow met some of my clients and this is where they got their story lines.

Being in as many homes as I have been in, I know there are real Desperate Housewives and I'm going to tell you about a few of them.

Most desperate housewives are spoiled and bored. Instead of putting their time to good use they try to entertain themselves by doing rather wild things. In the meantime, their husbands are working long hours so they could give these women everything they ask for.

These women will hit on their contractors; coaches, landscapers and whoever else will give them the time of day.

I tell my contractors all the time, to be polite, but keep your distance because I have seen a few of these girls in action! I tell them, if they seem a little too friendly, back off. Try not to be in the house without someone else because we have had several instances when these desperate housewives became a little too desperate.

One of these women lived in a beautiful home in Bergen County. We were renovating the master bath. Tony, a young, good-looking man who was about 31 years old was installing marble in the bathroom. Tony was from Florence, Italy. One day when he was working in the bath room, he heard a click behind him. He turned to see Susan, the homeowner, behind him completely naked. She locked the door.

Young Tony was scared and asked her to please open the door. "I'm happily married and my wife just gave birth to our first baby. Please let me out or I'll have to knock the door down". Susan continued coming towards him and telling him how much fun they could have together and no one will ever know about it. "You are so good looking and I love your accent. I really need you." Tony started walking towards the door.

He was ready to knock it down. Susan realized she didn't have a chance with him, so she let him out. Tony looked back at her and said, "I just wanted to do my job but you have to find someone else to finish the work". Tony never returned.

My second desperate housewife was from Connecticut. My guys were working on the first floor of the house on a library for the husband. This woman was always pleasant and left my guys alone to do their work.

One day the woman called me and said that when she was out shopping she happened to meet this extremely good-looking painter. On the back of his shirt was his name and company name. "He's so gorgeous, Roseann, I hired him."

"But Beth, we have a painter, we don't need another one and you don't even know if he knows how to paint. Beth, I don't hire people because they are good looking. I hire them if they are qualified to do the job."

Beth insisted and had him paint a spare room upstairs.

The next day when I arrived at the house, this young, good looking painter about 25 years old, was also there. Beth introduced him to me and asked me to select a paint color so Gus could paint the spare room. I selected a color and left, hoping that Gus, indeed, knew how to paint.

A couple of days later my general contractor, Hector, told me while they were all working downstairs, Gus was painting upstairs. The desperate housewife was serving my guys bottled water, while she served Gus cheese and crackers and wine. The following day, my workers heard Gus and Beth go into the Master Bedroom. They locked the door and they were in there for about forty minutes. Then they heard the shower go on. Later Gus and Beth emerged from the bedroom Gus went back to his painting and Beth went to pick up the children from school.

My third desperate housewife was celebrating her fortieth birthday at a well-known restaurant in Bergen County. She invited about 80 women from town to her party. The day after her party, I had to see a few clients from town and everyone was talking about the wild party they went to the night before.

Dorothy was dancing with a few of her female friends on the dance floor and they were French kissing one another. The male strippers put on quite a show and ended up going home with Dorothy and her friends. A few of the woman that I spoke to didn't expect it to be a party like this and they were horrified. Sometimes it is the ones you least expect.

THE BIG HOUSE ON THE HILL

The House On The Hill is a very special place. I guess the reason the house is so special to me is because the people who live in it are special people.

There is a history behind this house. This is the second time I decorated it. The first time was about eight years ago when a young couple contacted me and told me they had just bought a house and they wanted me to take a look at it. The house was very stately and had plenty of potential but it needed a tremendous amount of work.

The first time I met with my clients, the Real Estate broker who had sold them the house was with them. He was a real busybody and couldn't keep his mouth shut. I think he really wanted to decorate the house for them because whenever I made a suggestion, he contradicted me. I immediately put an end to this. I spoke to the homeowners when we left the house and told them if I were going to decorate the house for them, this crazy realtor couldn't be bothering me. They agreed that he was a real pain and didn't know what he was talking about and they got rid of him quickly.

We sat down and discussed what we were going to do to the house. We had to start by gutting most of it. We added a new kitchen, new bathrooms, and new floors. We converted the living room into a billiard room, knocked walls down and built a bar between the billiard room and the new office.

The project went on and on. We started July 27th and we were finished for this family to move in so the children could start school in September. The job went very smoothly and the house really turned out beautifully. The one thing I must say about this couple is they really listened and when people listen, things move along much faster. This man really knew that he wanted to do some really special things in the house.

At one point he had mentioned to me that he wanted us to put a fish tank in his new office. A couple of days later he called me to ask me the price of the shark tank. "Shark tank," I said. "I thought you just wanted a small fish tank."

"No, I need a price of a shark tank with built-ins surrounding it". Thousands of dollars later we had a thousand-gallon shark tank with shark swimming around in it. I have to admit it was pretty cool.

This couple lived in the house for about two years. One day I received a call from the wife who asked me if I knew anyone who would be interested in buying the house. She told me that her husband wasn't feeling well and that they had to downsize.

I immediately thought of another couple who I was decorating a home for on the other side of town. They were about to put on an addition because they needed more space. Coincidentally I had shown her the "house on the hill" while I was decorating it and she had always admired it. As a matter of fact, after seeing it, she always asked me how her big beautiful house was coming along, never thinking that someday this house would be hers.

I decided to contact them immediately. When I spoke to Kendall I was disappointed because she said I think we'll pass on it. The boys are still little and we would have to put them on the third floor alone. "Are you sure," I asked. "Yes, I'm sure." About twenty minutes later I received a call from her husband, Jeff who told me never call Kendall when something like this happens, call me directly "I want to see the house."

I got off of the telephone with Jeff and called the original homeowners and I made an appointment to bring Jeff right over. "It was love at first sight". As soon as Jeff saw it, he asked me to make an offer for him.

Suddenly, I was a realtor! I didn't mind doing it for them. I really liked both couples and I was happy I could help until I heard that the busybody realtor, who I didn't like, ended up making a ton of money collecting the Real Estate commission on the house that I really sold.

I truly was happy to help out. Kendall and Jeff bought the house immediately. There I was decorating the same beautiful house on the hill for the second time. They loved what I had done for the first owners, so most of the first floor stayed as is.

We made changes in the children's rooms because the new owners have two boys and two girls. We also changed the Master Bedroom to personalize it for Kendall and Jeff. We then went to the third floor, where we created Yankee Stadium for the boys. It's amazing! As you stand in the room you could almost hear the crowds in the stands cheer as the Yankees throw the opening pitch, to the Mets. The details of the crowds in the stands, the Yankee field and diamond, the players, the hot dog vendor and even the Yankee Stadium subway stop is so realistic that you feel as if you are really at Yankee Stadium.

The basement had never been touched. I had some great ideas; I just had to convince Jeff. I thought it would be great to put in an old fashion ice cream parlor, for the kids and the adults alike. Jeff wasn't sure at first but he finally went along with it.

When you go down the front staircase into the basement, you walk into an old-fashioned theatre lobby. This room has a fully stocked concession stand, a popcorn stand, and an old fashion ticket booth along with a handmade ticket lady.

From the lobby, you enter the theater. This room seats between 16 and 20 people. It's amazing. On the other side of the basement we incorporated a gym, and a very special children's play room and media room

I told the contractor to build a flat wall unit so we could paint a barn on it. The barn has a horse, a pig, their little girl and Jake, the dog. On the back wall we surprised Jeff by painting both Jeff and Kendall dressed as farmers, pitchfork and all. Their three other children are all painted doing farm chores on the closet doors. The last room is the wine cellar that I think is Jeff's favorite room. Only kidding!

Kendall and Jeff are very special to me. We have become very good friends. Last year, I decorated their second home at the shore and that was a lot of fun to do also.

They are very easy to work for. We seem to like the same things and they are not afraid to take a chance. If I make a suggestion they usually listen.

They are more than clients to me, they have become very close friends and they are a very big part of my life. They are fine people with high standards, good morals and I am proud to be a part of their lives. This house was really great fun and a great fit for this family. I am so happy to do the work that I do and to be able to turn these homes into magical places for people to live.

This house in particular is magical. How many homes have a Yankee Stadium, and ice cream parlor, an in-home theatre, there own barn, etc., etc., etc. This is a magical place to live and the people in it are just as magical.

THE CROOKED TREE

Christmas time is a very special time of year for me. Many of my clients love to decorate their homes for the holidays. I should say, they like me to decorate their homes for the holidays. Some of them have several trees in different rooms, garlands on staircase railings, and garlands on mantles, whatever it takes to make the house look festive and beautiful. People don't realize how many hours go into holiday decorating. This is very tedious work but Christmas is my favorite time of year and even though it's exhausting work, I love doing it.

In some of the big homes that I do, I bring a crew of people. There is no way that I could climb to decorate some of these twenty-plus foot trees by myself.

A few years ago, I was hired to decorate a house in Bergen County. I knew these people. I had worked for them before.

When my staff and I walked in, the Christmas tree in the entrance hall was already placed in its stand and the lights were already on the tree. This tree was about twenty-five feet tall but as soon as we looked at it we told the owner of the home that the tree was crooked. "We should straighten out the tree," I said. "No I don't want you to touch it. My husband wants it just the way it is."

"Could we get a rope, which won't show and we'll attach it to the column? I'm afraid if we don't do something with it, when we decorate, it will fall because of the weight on one side." She kept persisting that the tree was fine the way it was and she wanted us to decorate it that way.

We weren't very happy about this and told her so, but she persisted that it would be fine. She didn't want to upset her husband. She went on to say that their big holiday party was the next night and it had to get done. We persisted and she persisted and at the end, the client got her way. When we were finished with the tree, we were able to pull it over to one side so you couldn't really notice that it was crooked but I was really nervous about it.

We decorated her five mantles and did her beautiful staircase and landing and twelve hours later, we were done. It was a lot of work and we were all exhausted.

No sooner did I walk into my house and kick off my shoes when the telephone rang "Hello," I said. "Roseann, you have to come back. The tree fell. My husband is furious that you decorated a crooked tree."

When I heard this, I was furious. "Did you tell him you wouldn't let us straighten it out or tie it to the column?" I told her that we would be back the next morning, but that she had to let us take it out of the stand, the way we wanted to and re-do it.

When we arrived the next morning, her husband Angelo, a little tough guy who looked like he just came off of the set of The Soprano's was there and started screaming at me. I tried to tell him what had happened and that his wife wouldn't allow us to touch it because she thought he would get angry but he wouldn't listen to me. I told him it wasn't our fault the guy put it in the stand wrong.

While I was having a heated conversation with this guy. Jeremy, one of my contractors was laying under the tree shaking in his boots. He knew Angelo's family was involved in organized crime and I really think that he was afraid that Angelo was going to pull out a gun and shoot us. (I think he watches too much television.) He kept signaling to me to keep quiet, but at this point, I was really aggravated by the way Angelo was talking to me.

I knew this guy, I had decorated several of his previous homes and I wasn't afraid of Angelo. I told him that if he would leave us alone and let us do what we wanted to do in the first place, we could get the tree straightened out and redecorate it in time for the party. I said, "Angelo, next time tell the asshole who puts your trees in the stands to do it right." Angelo turned, looked at me and said, "I'm the asshole who put it in the stand."

I looked at Jeremy under the tree who was about to have a heart attack at this point. He saw his life flash before his eyes. He didn't know what was going to happen next. I turned towards Angelo and said calmly, I guess we all make mistakes sometimes, just let us fix your tree so you can have a good party. Angelo stormed out of the room, never looking back. We didn't see him for the remainder of the time that we were there.

Christmas trees are usually a lot of fun to decorate. This one was a little nerve racking, but, at the end, everything looked beautiful. I heard that the party was a great success. Jeremy was so happy that we didn't get "wacked".

"Music is magical."

THE LIMO WENT KA-BOOM

In my type of business you meet all kinds of people, in all walks of life. Sometimes I could work for people for a long while and never really know what type of work they do.

I usually, at the initial interview, review what they want me to do and I get back to them with a budget. If they say the budget is all right we start the project.

Some of my clients are very wealthy, some are just middle class, some just call me in for an hour to ask me to select colors. I work with all types of people.

Some of my clients are doctors and lawyers, plumbers, truck drivers, office workers, computer consultants, but one of them I guess was in an entirely different type of field. I thought that these people owned their own business, but I never really gave it much thought.

This particular client asked me to help with her wedding. She asked if I would help her coordinate her wedding because she had no one else to ask. She asked me to go and select a venue with her. We did and the following week, she asked if we could bring her future mother in law out to see the place. Of course, I said yes.

We met at her future mother in laws house where there was a big, black limo parked in front of the house. Jackie told me that this was her mother in laws limo and that we would be going with her. We had a really lovely day. We drove out and discussed the wedding plans. Her future mother in law was very sweet. She even told me that before she met her husband, she was in a convent, she wanted to become a nun. She was delightful. We looked at the reception location, went out to lunch, even did some shopping, and returned home. We had so much fun. I was so happy to meet her.

That evening, I was lying in bed and I heard my husband call to me to turn the television on. He said, "Turn the news on, Channel 7.

Your new friends are on TV." I didn't know what he was talking about. As I watched the news, I recognized the limo I had been in all day and I saw the driver. The news was reporting that this limo belonged to someone they referred to as, the John Gotti of New Jersey, and that the driver was his bodyguard. The reason this was on the news was because someone put a bomb under the limo. Thank God no one was in it. They blew it up.

My husband was shocked that I had been in that limo all day, I had been with these people and had been working for them for weeks and I didn't know who they were. "You could have been killed, don't you know who you are working for?" You could only ask so many questions and "Are you in the mafia, is not a question that you ask."

I found these people to be very nice and I'm there to decorate not to interrogate!

AW PRINTS

This next job was in Marshall, New Jersey. We were gutting out most of the house and then, we were going to rebuild and redecorate. We were working for a woman who watched every move we made.

We were replacing everything: walls, floors, carpets and bathrooms. Everything was going.

We finally got to the point where we put up the sheetrock, we patched and taped and spackled and we were about to paint the walls. We had left carpet down in the hallway just so that we wouldn't track dirt through the house but we knew we, were replacing it up in a few days. My client was such a terrible nag. She didn't want anything messed up so we made sure we were as neat as possible.

One day my two painters were at work. One of them opened the can of paint and the other didn't know that the lid was behind him on the floor. He stepped in it and walked on that rug with wet paint on his boots.

When he realized what he had done, he tried to clean it up but couldn't. Thinking quickly he took the lady's little dog and dipped her paws into the paint. He then put the dog down and had her run up and down the hallway with wet paws.

When the woman returned, he told her that the dog stepped in the paint. The woman picked up her little dog, kissed her and said, "You naughty little girl, what am I going to do with you?"

Fortunately I didn't hear about this episode until after the job was done. While I usually would not condone such dishonesty on the part of my contractors, in this case it was harmless. The rug was being replaced in a few days. I guess, sometimes, you have to think on your feet; but I guess in this case, your paws.

THE NURSERY (WHILE MOM WAS IN THE HOSPITAL)

Five years ago, one of my favorite clients called me to tell me that she was pregnant with her fourth child.

Roxanne never had a real nursery for any of her babies before because she lived in a little apartment in Queens. Since then, her husband had done very well in business and they bought a home in Bergen County. I had already decorated the house and I was thrilled when she called me to tell me about the new baby and the proposed nursery.

The one thing she was explicit about was that she didn't want to know the sex of the baby until it was born so I designed two rooms, one for a boy and one for a girl. We were set. I knew what I had to do and we were going to get it done while Mommy was in the hospital having the baby. I felt like I was on a reality TV show. It was very exciting.

Roxanne's husband was to call me, as soon as the baby was born, before he called anyone else so we could get started immediately. I was contacted even before the grandparents and we began working the next morning. They had a baby girl and we had the room completed when Mommy and baby came home.

I was at the house when they arrived and I was so proud and excited to show off the nursery. I brought Roxanne upstairs, with her mother. Even though I had seen the room, when I opened the door to show them for the first time, this was one of those magical moments. The three of us stood at the doorway speechless and crying. This really would have been a great reality TV show.

The walls were a soft flush pink with sheep and cows running through the meadows and hand painted pink and white checkerboard outside of the picture frame molding. It was all so sweet.

We built a lovely white dollhouse and placed it on top of a column behind the cattycornered crib. We also use it for a night-light. The crisp white organdy curtains with pink ribbons and home made baby wreaths with flowers dress up the room.

This was definitely my favorite nursery. Some rooms you just love more than others. This one will always be magical to me. I never duplicated this room because I thought this room should just belong to Madison. Mommy's dream finally came true, she finally had her fairy tale nursery for one of her babies.

This room put a big smile on everyone's face. Doing this nursery gave me much joy.

THE COFFIN

When clients ask what style I like the best, I always answer I personally love transitional but I could do anything.

Well, this didn't hold true in this particular case. About ten years ago, I was asked to do a job in Orangeburg, New York. I decorated the house and things seemed to be going pretty well until they asked me to decorate their teenage daughter's room.

They told me to do whatever it was that she wanted.

This girl was weird! I found her to be a very dark, demonic type of person. She wore black nail polish and black lipstick. She had spiked orange-looking hair. She was very freaky.

The thing I found most weird about her was she wanted me to get her a coffin to sleep in.

I have been asked to do a lot of strange things but never something like this. What shocked me more than anything, was that her parents went along with this very strange behavior.

I wouldn't go along with it. I told them I didn't work with coffins. She ended up settling for a black and white bedroom with a black Formica bed.

It's very hard to work in some client's homes. Some people are so normal and then there are others who are just so very strange.

DECORATING EMERGENCIES

The term decorating emergency is not a term you can find in the dictionary nor in any decorating book. You won't hear the term if you go to design school but it is definitely a part of a decorator's life.

For years my husband and children, have been trying to understand exactly what the term means. A decorating emergency could be almost anything. It could happen anytime of the day or night. It can happen when the decorator is on vacation or working with another client.

A decorating emergency is anything a client believes is so important that he or she should wake you up in the middle of the night to tell you all about it.

I realize that people entrust me with decisions about their homes. I truly appreciate the fact that they have so much faith in me that they feel they cannot make a decision without me.

Sometimes it just becomes a little crazy. I don't want to come across sounding as if I don't care about my clients. This couldn't be further from the truth but some times I get calls at ridicules times of the night, during holiday dinners and when I am on vacations. I guess this is my fault because I always try to make myself available for my clients, however it would be nice if the decorating emergencies took place between nine and five.

Not too long ago, I was rushed to the hospital. The doctors did not know exactly what was wrong with me. I was losing a lot of blood and they had to decide if they were going to put me in intensive care or if they were going to give me blood transfusions. All they knew at this time was that I was very sick.

In the midst of all this commotion one of my newer clients, who only hired me to select colors for her home, called my office. My daughter, Stacey who works with me told her that I was rushed to the hospital and how serious my condition was. The client seemed to just ignore what Stacey was saying and demanded that she have my room number at the hospital. (This was not to send me flowers.) She wanted to call me so I could select her paint colors.

Stacey was shocked by her reaction and told her that I could not be bothered with this right now. Mrs. X demanded that I be contacted because this was a decorating emergency that had to be taken care of immediately.

Stacey offered to help her select the colors because she is also a decorator, but Mrs. X refused. She called the office for days and finally said that she could not wait any longer. She asked Stacey if we could recommend another decorator. Stacey told her that we weren't in the business of referring other decorators.

I have to admit, this never happened to me before. My other clients were very understanding and very concerned.

My family tells me not to take my telephone on vacations but I try to explain to them that I would rather take five or ten minutes out while I'm on vacation to take care of a little problem so when I go home I don't go home to a big disaster.

To tell you the truth, it does not bother me when a client calls me to ask me a question. I know myself that when I'm lying in bed at night, I'm going over the projects that I am working on. It's not the type of job that you can just turn off. I guess that I love what I do so much that even if I'm on a beach someplace, I'm always thinking of my work.

In most cases my clients are the best. I love working with them and talking to them whenever they want to talk to me. A home is usually a person's most valuable possession and I understand why they feel that everything that happens is so important and is a decorating emergency.

Decorating emergencies are what keeps my business alive.

"Abstract Art is abstract."
"I am no Picasso or Van Gogh, I am just a person
who enjoys decorating, painting, and creating for my clients."

Art

Art means different things to different people. Art is very personal and this is why, when it is time for us to purchase art for a client's home, I insist that they are involved in this process.

About thirty years ago I had a client in Fairlawn, New Jersey. She was a lovely lady who had very good taste and a good eye for color. After decorating her home, she asked if I would take her shopping for artwork. We shopped several days but we just couldn't find anything that she really liked. She had a very contemporary home and told me she loved color but she just couldn't find any painting with the right colors.

One day, while we were shopping she said to me, "Why don't you paint me something with the perfect colors". I looked at her and told her because I never painted anything before. When she put this thought into my head I started thinking maybe I could paint something for her. The next morning I went to Pearl Paints and bought some canvas and paints and I decided I was going to give this a try.

The first few paintings that I did were horrible but I persisted and I started to feel very comfortable and created my own style of painting. It really was all about color and texture and movement. Once I started painting, I couldn't put the brush down. I loved it.

I painted a picture for her and brought it to her house. My heart was in my throat. Of course, the colors were perfect but I didn't know what she was going to think. I was really very nervy back then to think that I could do something like this without any training and no experience.

When I brought her the painting she loved it and asked if I would do a second painting for another room. I was completely shocked when she told me she taught art and thought these painting were great. I knew she was a teacher, but had I known that she was an art teacher,

I would have been completely intimidated and I would have never attempted this.

Since that time my art has improved. I have created a new art form that I call Abstract Venetian Art. Many of my clients have commissioned me to do a piece for their home or office. As a matter of fact, just recently, I did a doctors office in Park Ridge and second office in Paramus. These offices look like art galleries. The doctor bought about 12 pieces of my art for the first office and about 20 for the second office. The office environment is very peaceful and I was told by one of the nurses she thinks when the patients sit there and look at the art it actually lowers their blood pressure. Last week I was at the new office and one of the Doctor's told me how much she loved the office. She went on to say that her favorite thing in the office were the paintings. She said that my painting reminded her of Jackson Pollock's paintings. I always admired his style so this was a huge compliment.

As I said before, art is very personal. Some people believe that to qualify as "art", a painting must have flowers or scenery in it. Abstract art is abstract. People see what they want to see.

I was entertaining at home one night and my guest, started telling me what they saw when they looked at my paintings. One man who was also an artist saw Jesus on the Cross and someone else saw a baby in his mother's arms.

I'm no Picasso or Vincent Van Gogh. I'm just a person who enjoys every second of every day decorating, painting and creating for my clients. I hope they enjoy my work as much as I enjoy doing it. My paintings are just an extension of what I do and what I enjoy doing.

"Accessories are necessities."

THE UNINVITED GUEST

My decorating has taken me in many different directions. Not only do I decorate homes and offices but I am very often asked to decorate parties, weddings, and many different events. I guess this also makes me a party planner.

One of my most favorite and most memorable weddings was a home garden wedding that took place in my own back yard.

When my daughter Shawn became engaged to Bill, they came and told me they would like a garden wedding. Of course, I asked, whose garden? I knew what they were talking about but I also knew what was involved. Garden weddings are beautiful but you just don't know what to expect. I knew I couldn't say no and I was really excited to have it at home. I would have full control, I wouldn't have to take orders from anyone and I could do anything I wanted.

The wedding was planned. It was to take place on September 18th. The gown was selected, the caterers gave us a food tasting, the tent and furniture was rented, and the band was hired. The hundreds of flowers were planted in the garden. Our guests were invited but unfortunately we had an uninvited guest, FLOYD (Hurricane Floyd).

The tent was installed on Tuesday and Wednesday, the week of the wedding. It was a lot of work because we had it installed on top of our swimming pool. It was a huge job. The tent was finally ready to be decorated and that's when we heard on the news that Hurricane Floyd was on its way.

The tent company refused to help me decorate because of the storm warning. We had to wait and see if Floyd was really coming and how hard he was going to hit.

On Thursday, Floyd hit with a force. The winds were so strong that we thought that we were going to loose the tent. The inside of the tent was flooded. The carpeting was destroyed. But what's the old saying, "The show must go on".

After the rehearsal dinner on Thursday evening, with the help of the bridal party, I started to decorate the tent by candlelight. That night I prayed that it looked good the next morning.

Friday morning it was still drizzling but the wind stopped. I set up the tables and chairs and continued to pray that the power would go back on. How could we have a party without power?

Saturday morning, still no power but we had lots of sunshine. The horse and carriage was to arrive to take Shawn and my husband to the church at noon. The caterer's arrived with their tale of woe. They had been flooded and all of their cooking equipment was under water. They were supposed to do all of the cooking and prep work in my freshly painted garage. Unfortunately this was not going to happen.

At eleven o'clock our power went back on. Thank you God!

The caterers used my kitchen to prepare 120 meals and it worked out beautifully.

We had the cocktail party in our garden room and on my deck that was completely covered with white tenting. Shawn was so calm. She went to the A&P to pick up some lemons for the bartender in her make up and veil. She wasn't worried about anything. She knew I along with her sister Stacey would take care of everything, which we did.

The horse and carriage arrived. Shawn looked like a princess. The little country church was charming. The ceremony was lovely and everyone returned home. People were telling us, how beautiful everything looked. The cocktail party was wonderful.

When the sun went down, the host announced, candlelight dinner will be served and the side drapes were raised displaying the interior of the tent filled with hundreds of candles and white and cream colored roses. At each end of the tent was a stone cherub holding pots filled with roses and ivory. On the evergreen trees surrounding the tent, were hundreds of clear twinkling lights. It felt like Disney World. It was truly spectacular. The music played and the party went on and on. We didn't have to get out at any special time. We were home.

As the guests exited we had two large farmers baskets filled with baby pears, wrapped in clear cellophane with ribbon on them that said, "Shawn and Bill, what a great pair".

Everything was perfect, the wedding was over but the memories will remain forever.

Since that time I have done many outdoor weddings, Communions, graduations etc. Luckily my clients always have good weather. I guess God hands it out to those He knows can handle it.

There's nothing like a home garden wedding. I recommend it to everyone.

IN THE BEGINNING

For years, one of my dreams was to open an infant's clothing store and I was going to call it "In The Beginning". This never happened for me but several years ago I did something that made up for it.

An organization that helped unwed mothers and abused women contacted me and asked if I would help them. John, one of my old contractors gave them my name and number and told them to call me.

The organization needed to raise money to help them keep it's home open. A wealthy gentleman from Allendale, New Jersey owned several stores in the area. He was willing to allow the organization to use one of these stores rent free to sell merchandise to raise money for these needy women

When they called to ask me to help them decorate the store, I suggested that maybe they could open an infant's resale clothing store. They wouldn't have to invest any money to buy merchandise and if they could contact the right people, they might collect beautiful merchandise.

Of course, this is where I came in. I contacted my clients who were very happy to donate clothing they had saved from when they had infants. Some of the outfits were used only once or twice. Some of the outfits were never worn. The organization collected clothes and children's furniture and cribs and bassinets and accessories; everything you would see in a nursery. Everything just clicked!

My contractor, John donated his services and fixed up the shop. My painter Jeremy did a fantastic job painting soft clouds on the walls and ceiling. I made lovely white organdy curtains with ribbons and one of my showrooms donated new flooring. The store was ready to go.

The women knew that I had always wanted to open an infant store and asked me what I was going to call my store. When I told them "In

The Beginning", they asked if they could use my name. I thought this was a great idea and a wonderful compliment and it truly helped my dream become a reality.

We ordered a sign for in front of the store that looked like a cloud and had "In the Beginning" painted on it.

We had a grand opening and hundreds of people showed up. Newspaper reporters came and took pictures and we had write-ups in all of the newspapers.

The store was a great success. Aside from raising money to help keep this home running, it served a second purpose. Every woman who resided in the home had to give a certain amount of time working in the store. It helped the women keep motivated and they also got paid for the time they worked.

This was such a rewarding experience for me. It was such a good feeling knowing that I could help these people. It is so important to give a little of yourself. It helps others but it also feels so good to know that you did something to help change someone's life.

"I love to go out on my deck early in the morning to listen to the silence and then the birds seem to suddenly wake up and start singing in the trees."

A DECORATOR'S TEN COMMANDMENTS PLUS ONE

1   Thou shalt not forget to pay your decorator.
2   Thou shalt not take advice from everyone in the family or neighborhood. (Trust the decorator.)
3   Thou shalt not buy furniture off a truck that's parked on the street (because it's so cheap).
4   Thou shalt not allow your children to draw all over your furniture with Magic Markers and then tell your decorator the furniture didn't hold up.
5   Thou shalt not be afraid to use dark colors when painting.
6   Thou shalt not cheap out before you complete a room. The window treatment, which is the last thing to complete the room, is probably the most expensive element of the room. It's like putting on a beautiful dress without a piece of jewelry. It's not complete without it.
7   Thou shalt not call your decorator with a million questions and then think that she shouldn't charge you for this time.
8   Thou shalt not keep changing your mind. Make a decision and stick with it.
9   Thou shalt not call saying it's a "decorating emergency" unless the house is falling down.
10 Thou shalt not call after hours. Be considerate, your decorator also needs time to herself.
+1 Accessorize.

My CONTRACTORS

My contractors are very important to me. I have been working with the same people for years. They know what I like and what I expect from them. I just have to tell them once and they understand.

I have painters, faux finishers, muralists, architects, builders, carpet and custom carpet people, window treatment people, etc., etc. Each and every one of my contractors are artist and always make me proud of their fine workmanship. I truly would be nothing without my contractors. They are all incredible to work with and each and every one of them has become a big part of my family.

Working with them makes my life so much easier and less stressful. They know what I expect from them and I always get what I expect!

Thanks guys for always being at my side.

My CLOSING BLESSING

Thank you God for my life, for my family and for my decorating. Yes, of course, I have had bad things happen to me, like everyone else but you have always helped me through them.

You have given me so many wonderful blessings, experiences along with the talents you gave me. I couldn't have done anything without you.

You have taught me that decorating is a blessing. You help me make people's dreams come true. You help me make people see beauty. You help me make people happy.

There is so much beauty in my business. Instead of focusing on fighting with people or making deals, or ripping people off like so many other businesses, I am blessed to deal with pretty colors, beautiful furniture and fabrics and being able to see the smiles on peoples faces when they first see the room I did for them. How lucky am I?

You were very generous with me when you gave out blessings. I am so lucky I could design and decorate a home, or play the piano, paint a picture or write a book that makes people laugh and cry. I am blessed because of you.

Thank you God so much and may you always be proud of the way I'm using the talents you blessed me with.

Your loving friend and Decorating Servant,
Roseann

$\mathcal{A}$ FEW WORDS FROM
ROSEANN'S CLIENTS

The first time I met Roseann Kearney, she rang my door bell, stepped into my living room and said, "Can you pick up the other end of this couch, I think it should be over there!" With Roseann holding up one end and my husband Frank holding the other, we turned the sofa around and placed it down on the other side of the room.

In that instant, our long, rectangular shaped, bland, white walled living room felt instantly warmer . . . cozier . . . more "homey." We knew then and there, this would be the beginning of a wonderful relationship.

Roseann understood that a house filled with beautiful things is not necessarily a home . . . that decorating is all about the people who live there, not the things that happen to be there. Her love of family, of children and pets, her compassion for all her clients who inevitably end up as her friends, make her like a captivating piece of art, unique and inspiring.

Roseann has brought beauty and warmth to the homes and families she has touched. She not only decorated our home, she has decorated our lives.

Diane and Frank Lento

The day I met Roseann, I knew she would be more than a decorator!! I had just moved to this house far away from my family and friends. The best part is that I was all alone with three children under three! The house was beautiful but well for lack of a better word . . . boring. I was going crazy looking at all those beige walls with three kids all day, so I took a friends advice and called Roseann.

She rang the door bell that first day and while I was going to open the door my 2 year old twins dumped a box of Cheerios onto their baby brother's Exersaucer. The dog and the kids were going crazy. Roseann walked in and just laughed and I knew that instant that she was the perfect fit for this crazy family!

Since that first "crazy" day all those years ago, Roseann has not only beautifully decorated 4 of our houses; she has become a part of our family! Not only is she an incredible decorator, but she is an incredible friend, always here for us whenever we need her.

She is always the first one to reach out to us when life throws us a curve ball. When I moved to this area I was all alone, but in the chaos of my life, I not only found someone who could turn my houses into homes, I found my "New Jersey Mother."

Kathryn Grifonetti

Knowing Roseann for over 15 years we have seen her beautiful work as a decorator and her amazing flair for party planning. We have had the pleasure of working with Roseann and her clients on any many projects and have seen the effort she puts in to each and every one. Having her as your decorator is like hiring someone who will be there for you 24-7

We have had the pleasure of personally having Roseann plan our wedding renewal celebration. Every detail was filled with love and she made that day a magical moment in our life, one that will last forever.

Her love and dedication to her field is commendable. Roseann walked into our store a stranger; and today she is indeed a very special friend that we love.

Gaye & Sam Levine
G. Fried Carpet & Design

We have worked with Roseann for the past ten years, and two houses. Roseann's talent goes way beyond a "typical" decorator. She has saved us a lot of money and time, while always respecting our vision. Maybe, most importantly is the joy she brings to a project, we laugh and have so much fun together. To us, Roseann is family.

Lisa and Dan Schwartz

As a construction company, you always want your work to look its best and Roseann has a way of helping ours shine. We have a long time relationship with Roseann, she has recommended us on many occasions and we always recommend her to our customers as well.

She has a way of really listening to her customers, finding out what they are thinking and making it all happen. There are times when she will describe her ideas and I am thinking how the heck will this ever work and by the end, it is exactly how she described it. She is truly an artist and makes every project unique.

We do not only work with Roseann on a professional level but we are also one of her clients. Anything Roseann has helped us with in our own home is always complimented on.

It is always a pleasure to work with Roseann, not only will the finished project be beautiful but she will also keep you laughing with all her funny stories.

Andrew and Karen Greene

Roseann is a wonderfully creative designer who is very knowledgeable in the current trends of interior design. What makes Roseann unique is her ability to understand her clients' vision and guide them in the right direction.

I am overwhelmed by even minor design decisions and my natural instinct is to ignore the project. Without Roseann, I would have continued to live in an unfinished, dated and sparsely furnished house. Roseann encouraged me to focus and instituted a workable plan of attack. Roseann is my friend who happens to be a great decorator. She has an uncanny ability to know what I want when I can't even describe it myself.

I trust Roseann implicitly and know that she will do her best and be the best.

Randy Nassau

CPSIA information can be obtained at www.ICGtesting.com
Printed in the USA
LVOW041739100112

263232LV00002B/82/P